I0791524

Life or deathocracy

The choice is yours

D.C. Link

Archway Publishing books may be ordered through booksellers or by contacting:

Archway Publishing
1663 Liberty Drive
Bloomington, IN 47403
www.archwaypublishing.com
844-669-3957

ISBN: 978-1-6657-3029-7 (sc)
ISBN: 978-1-6657-3030-3 (hc)
ISBN: 978-1-6657-3031-0 (e)

Library of Congress Control Number: 2022917158

Print information available on the last page.

Archway Publishing rev. date: 01/18/2023

If at any time I declare concerning a nation or a
kingdom, that I will pluck up and break down and
destroy it, **8** and if that nation, concerning which I have
spoken, turns from its evil, I will relent of the disaster
that I intended to do to it. **9** And if at any time I declare
concerning a nation or a kingdom that I will build and
plant it, **10** and if it does evil in my sight, not listening
to my voice, then I will relent of the good that I had
intended to do to it.

—Jeremiah 18:7-10

CONTENTS

INTRODUCTION

There is no shortage of concerned Americans, and you have been one of them since you are reading this book. Although concerned, you may question whether deathocracy is a real thing.

Before answering whether *deathocracy* exists, the cause of extensive "patriotic concern" needs to be examined. Without question, the year 2020 was like no other in American politics and culture, but could it be a culmination of something that "We the People" have given party to?

In the 2000s I began to notice a rapidly degrading moral standard of not just the public order, but also the federal government of the United States. Curiosity drove me to research what the United States was intended to be, how it was supposed to operate, and what made it such a great nation. What I found was convicting for me and, quite honestly... shocking. As time went on and patterns of degeneration became more defined, it was clear that something ominous was taking hold of us. That "something" is precisely what the founders warned us about and will fully dismantle our sovereignty if allowed to continue. Since dismantling any nation's sovereignty is death, the only name the process can be given is *deathocracy*. **So, yes, *deathocracy* is real.**

The next question is whether *deathocracy* is the same as the *culture of death*.

The *culture of death* is more of a critical ingredient of *deathocracy than its comparative*. The *culture of death* implies the cultivation and glorification of death. It can also be described as the preference for wickedness and dirtiness over wholesomeness and dignity. The evidence of our declining culture is mainly what is considered entertainment and justice and whether justice and governments are viewed as entertainment. As culture spirals further downward, perception of justice and government is increasingly crafted by entertainment, and entertainment becomes more abhorrent. As any society becomes more in tune with entertainment and less in tune with reality, that society becomes more *suspicious.* The *culture of suspicion* is both the by-product and the fuel for the *culture of death* that prevails throughout American society. The *culture of suspicion* is the biological mother of societal division because it's impossible to be united with those you suspect.

Deathocracy is institutional, while the *cultures of death* and the *culture of suspicion* remain a commercial and public issue for politicians and oligarchs to derive *deathocratic* powers from. As culture cultivates the kindle, *deathocracy* is the fire that burns a nation to the ground. A *deathocratic* society knowingly and unknowingly acts as the arsonist of its own country. *Deathocracy* is the legislation of death from the top and then carrying it out in blind faith from the bottom.

Readers must know that this book is not written to be a philosophical journey but instead an uncomfortable conviction of patriotic duty. Right now, the stakes are higher than ever in history, and the odds for us are far worse than in the Revolutionary War. In this book, you will find no support or political slant towards or against any group, party, or person. **This particular work is about a deep down inside truth that no one else will talk about, yet the only truth that needs to be discussed.**

PART 1

Charters of Justice

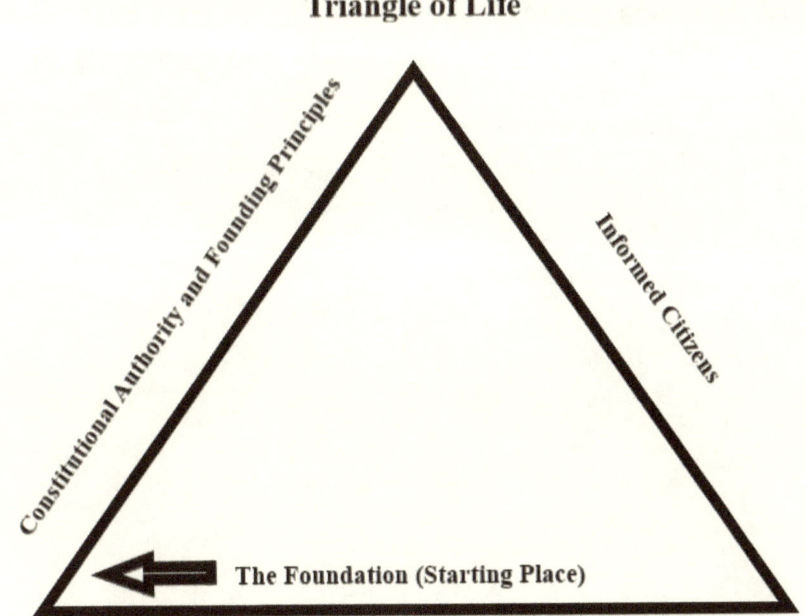

I pledge *allegiance* to the flag of the United States of America, and to the republic for which it stands, one nation, under God, with liberty and justice for all.

CHAPTER 1

The Power of Principle

"Whereas it is the duty of all Nations to acknowledge the providence of Almighty God, to obey his will, to be grateful for his benefits, and humbly to implore his protection and favor—and whereas both Houses of Congress have by their joint Committee requested me to recommend to the People of the United States a day of public thanksgiving and prayer to be observed by acknowledging with grateful hearts the many signal favors of Almighty God especially by affording them an opportunity peaceably to establish a form of government for their safety and happiness."

—**George Washington**[1]

In the woods of western Pennsylvania in 1755, an American volunteer officer took on legendary status for salvaging a British force of 1300+ from destruction by the hands of the French and their Native American allies.[2] George Washington, who served in the thick of the battle and yet physically unscathed, allegedly had bullet holes in his coat. As with many successes in his life, when George Washington was asked about this particular battle, Washington always gave credit to the hand of providence (Barton).[3]

While leading the United States military and militia to Revolutionary War victory, General Washington continued to mirror what was expected of the American character of that time and for the years to come. After the Treaty of Paris in September of 1883, the official end of the war, George Washington, at that time, possessed more power than any American then or since. He was the commander in chief of all armed forces, extremely popular and held a high degree of trust among the American society and government. With that power and confidence at his disposal, he resigned his command and returned to private life. The release of that great power set several precedents for personal character and public service etiquette.

Washington had some political experience but was known more as a military leader. Like many founders, he was sympathetic to a federal national design. He believed a more defined central government was necessary for the success of a nation over the confederation style of government instituted at the time under the Articles of Confederation.

In 1787, after the American Confederacy was found in need of review, Washington was called out of private life and back into public service to lead the Constitutional Convention. As a result of the Convention, the Constitution was ratified in September of 1789, thirteen years after the Declaration of Independence. With the opening of **"We the People of the United States, to form a more perfect Union…"** the Constitution becomes the most republican and *timeless* legal document created by man. The United States then takes on the highest form of government and the hardest one to maintain.

Because of Washington's steadfast and continued leadership, he was deluged by colleagues to run for the new position of president of the US, then elected unanimously by the delegates.

Washington's presidency was arguably the most difficult of all presidencies, and it's hard to imagine anyone but him capable. Some initial challenges were to recover from the state of affairs caused by the duration of the Confederacy, including paying down the war debt and putting down a whiskey rebellion. The constitutional United States faced many significant challenges during the Washington presidency, including Islamic terrorism, French hostility, British control of western territories, and political infighting. Washington remained steadfast in upholding constitutional authority and set many invaluable precedents for the American republic.

As the first president winds down his second term, he writes a farewell speech that summarizes American principles and a foundational warning to the electorate and the elected. Though the address is often called political advice today, today's America is proving that it should have been heeded with a high degree of seriousness. The uber-enlightened patriot's farewell address can be found easily online at senate.gov under the art and history tab. A summary of American principles from Washington is below, all from his farewell address[4] except for the last one:

➢ Be forgiving to your leaders.
➢ Obey the government and respect the Constitution's authority as a maxim of liberty.

  • Protect the Constitution's principles from alterations that will steal its energy.
  • Obstruction of the execution of the law is fatally destructive.
  • Branches and officials should stay within their constitutional sphere.

➢ The spirit of party can become your worst enemy and will usually produce factions that lead to despotism. (Washington ran and served both terms without party affiliation.)
➢ The Union should be the primary object of your patriotism.
➢ Honesty is always the best policy, both in public and private matters.
➢ Guard your love of liberty and know that there is never a time to abandon it
➢ Preserve the state resources by using them sparingly, and by cultivating peace, and avoiding debt.
➢ Extend commercial relations with other countries and have as few political connections with them as possible. (The founding collective intended neutrality.)

> ➢ Always seek the favor and protection (providence) of God by being as decent and morally sound as possible in public and private matters.
> ➢ Avoid overgrown military establishments because they are dangerous to liberty and hostile to republican liberty while always remembering to be ready (military-industrial complex was not a phrase then, and "being ready" is lined out precisely in the US Constitution and the Bill of Rights)
> ➢ The common defense of the US should be based on state-run, Congress-regulated militias (This is also constitutional and is the purpose of the Second Amendment. More specifics in later chapters.)[5]

As mentioned, the above was echoed by the founders as a collective, especially the more prominent ones like John Adams, Samuel Adams, James Madison, James Monroe, Benjamin Franklin, and Thomas Jefferson. The redundancy of the above from the founders and framers means that they make up the core of our defining American principles.

Thomas Jefferson, an activist for American republicanism and respect for constitutional authority, felt a personal charge to tie American character and virtue to the principles paraphrased earlier. Thomas Jefferson, the primary author of the Declaration of Independence and third president of the United States under the Constitution, had given the better part of fifty years of his life to public service. He served at various levels of government in Virginia, including governor during a portion of the Revolutionary War, wrote many of the Virginia laws, and fathered the Virginia Statute of Religious Freedom. He was sent as a diplomat to foreign countries, served as secretary of state, vice president, and president of the US, and is one of the most prolific founders of the United States.

This accomplished statesman not only publicly fought attempts to extend government overreach but also the institution of slavery, which he considered an abomination before and after the Revolutionary War (Barton 16).[6] Jefferson was a seasoned veteran in the war against slavery and a pioneer in the colonies for the abolition movement. Jefferson proposed laws in Virginia that opposed slavery at the pain of facing ostracism from his fellow Virginians. When he was president, he promoted and signed the Act Prohibiting Importation of Slaves into law, making it a federal crime to import enslaved people. It wasn't until thirteen presidents and just over fifty years after Thomas Jefferson left office that slavery finally became illegal in all states, which initiated the bloody conflict Jefferson warned about repeatedly.

Jefferson was also an advocate for certain guaranteed protections, like freedom of speech, religion, habeas corpus, fair trials, etc., but so were most founders. Jefferson was a legal and government genius but only made recommendations after reading the complete draft of the Constitution in France.[7] The "Bill of Rights," which comprises the first ten amendments of the Constitution, was added to garner ratification from "anti-federalist" run states. Many framers (primarily federalist thinkers) who argued against the insertion of the Bill of Rights believed that all necessary rights were implied in the Constitution and that the states were responsible for further protection. The so-called "anti-federalist" conditions prevailed in the case, so the rights were added. Jefferson had a tiny hand in the Bill of Rights but was on the side of certain protections, and particularly from a standing army instead of a militia, and religious coercion from government institutions.

Many think of Virginia's Statute for Religious Freedom, a legislative masterpiece, as the basis of the "freedom of religion" clause in the First Amendment. However, Article VI Section 3, which states "no religious test shall be required for Qualification," makes the "make no law respecting an establishment of religion" portion of the First Amendment somewhat of a necessary redundancy. Both the constitutional clause and the First Amendment clause were written to protect the individual, the government, and the nation from institutionally coerced religious practice or belief.

Caution in this regard, held by the founders in general, was justified as Jefferson wrote in Virginia's statute for religious freedom:

"That the impious presumption of legislators and rulers, civil as well as ecclesiastical, who, being themselves but fallible and uninspired men, have assumed dominion over the faith of others, setting up their own opinions and modes of thinking as the only true and infallible, **and as such endeavoring to impose them on others, hath established and maintained false religions over the greatest part of the world and through all time."**[8]

The statute was intended to protect Virginians from religious imposition and coercion. The First Amendment and Article VI Section 3 of the Constitution both echoed that same sentiment. Not only do they declare protected religious practice, but also that our rights come from a Holy God, not man. The intent of Jefferson with the Virginia statute and the framers during the Convention was that if our rights are from man, then man can take them away.

The founders, including Jefferson, were very clear about the role God takes in government and yet very careful not to assume the position of God in defining the role of government. They were also adamant that a nation needed God's hand of providence (protection) to be prosperous and happy. The founders and framers undoubtedly believed and professed that to secure the blessings of liberty, and the right to pursue happiness, then a country must seek the favor of God and His divine protection (providence at the time).

The *need to seek God* principle is as clear, if not more evident, as the *religious freedom principle*. The final statement of the Declaration of Independence, written primarily by Jefferson, is "And for the support of this Declaration, **with a firm Reliance on the Protection of divine Providence,** we mutually pledge to each other our Lives, our Fortunes, and our sacred Honor," leaving little question about the revolutionaries' stance on God's role as judge over the heart of man and nations.

Thomas Jefferson served as our third president of the United States for two very productive terms. Jefferson was an accomplished and constitutionally sound president and leader. President Jefferson further echoed what should be heralded as fundamental American principles in his inaugural address. The inaugural speeches can easily be found on the Avon Law website and should be no less required reading than George Washington's farewell address and the Constitution. Below are some vital points that could add up to a summary of the principles that Jefferson advocated for and upheld to the extent of his authority in his fifty or so years of public service. The first eight principles are from his first inaugural[9] and second inaugural[10] addresses and the last two are supported by quotes from other prominent founders:

- Republics require the passive obedience of their citizens and their leaders.
- Peace, commerce, and genuine friendship with all nations, entangling alliances with none.
- Our defense should be militia-based (with a navy) (Also implied in the body of the Constitution and reinforced by the Second Amendment).
- We are all republicans, and we are all federalists. (This is speaking to the danger of parties.)
- The Constitution must be upheld and referred to in all difficult decisions.
- When the press abuses its freedom, it destroys its usefulness and threatens its existence. It is up to the citizens to defend against the unruliness and defamation of the media (as with any right, abusing them is an excellent way to lose them).
- The government must suppress and disband its useless institutions to protect the fruit of the citizen's labor (government should be efficient), and the national debt should be kept small.
- Nations should always seek the favor and protection of God, and the Revolution had the hand of God's providence and guidance over it.
- A significant and permanent standing army is dangerous to the United States for various reasons and should be avoided by using the more superior mechanism of defense, which is militias.[11]
- If we are to remain a self-governed republic, citizens must be informed.[12]
- Industry (producing something) is how capital is created, and a competitive free market is how it is obtained; debt (public and

private), banking systems, and the replacement of gold and silver with baseless paper is detrimental to the US. *Capitalism as a system instead of a competitive free market will never end well*[13]

➤ Be industrious and not look for the next big thing.

➤ **To keep a republic, those chosen to lead must be God-fearing and morally principled. Those selected to govern are a direct reflection of those who elected them to lead.**

➤ There will always be those who seek to destroy liberty and degenerate society; you should always be ready to fend against them.

    o "The liberties of our country, the freedoms of our civil Constitution are worth defending at all hazards; it is our duty to defend them against all attacks. We have received them as a fair inheritance from our worthy ancestors. They purchased them for us with toil and danger and expense of treasure and blood. It will bring a mark of everlasting infamy on the present generation— enlightened as it is—if we should suffer them to be wrested from us by violence without a struggle or to be cheated out of them by the artifices of designing men."
    —**Samuel Adams**[14]

➤ Democracy is dangerous; that is why we are a republic, even though it requires the most to keep.

    o "I do not say that democracy has been more pernicious on the whole, and in the long run, than monarchy or aristocracy. Democracy has never been and never can be so durable as aristocracy or monarchy; but while it lasts, it is bloodier than either.... Remember, democracy never lasts long. It soon wastes, exhausts, and murders itself. There never was a democracy yet that did not commit suicide. It is in vain to say that democracy is less vain, less proud, less selfish, less ambitious, or less avaricious than aristocracy or monarchy. It is not true, in fact, and nowhere appears in history. Those passions are the same in all men, under all forms of simple government, and when unchecked, produce the same effects of fraud, violence, and cruelty. When clear prospects are opened before vanity, pride, avarice, or ambition, for their easy gratification, it is hard for the most considerate philosophers and the most conscientious moralists to resist the temptation. Individuals have conquered themselves. Nations and large bodies of men, never."

**—John Adams,
The Letters of John and Abigail Adams**[15]

As the founders warned, the legislation of morality is a dangerous form of tyranny, however, there must be morality in all legislation for a nation to stand. The decision of what is moral should be made from a foundation of principles that honor God. What makes the United States what it is, is that our founding principles give us the best chance of happy and sustained self-government. These principles could have only come from men with the highest moral character and virtue, and they are principles that we must be united in.

I pledge allegiance to the flag of the United States of America, **and to the *republic* for which it stands,** one nation, under God, with liberty and justice for all.

CHAPTER 2

The Reality of Republicanism

"The republican is the only form of government which is not eternally at open or secret war with the rights of mankind."

—**Thomas Jefferson**[16]

The Constitutional republic is not only the highest form of government; it's the only form of government that genuinely preserves liberty. There was one single purpose of the Constitutional Convention, and that was to federalize the states under one strong republican government. This truth is evident in Article IV, Section 4 of the US Constitution, declaring, "The United States shall guarantee to every state in this union a *republican* form of government.." The Constitution's wording is not only proof of republican intention but is also the supreme law of the land. That means that republicanism is not optional, but it's a mandate.

It is easy to say that the United States Constitution is a masterpiece, but it's hard to grasp why it is a masterpiece entirely. The Constitution is so simple yet so profound. It covers everything it needs to, and not a touch more. Since 1789, the original body has not been altered, and it need not be. What the Constitution does not guarantee or make provision for is as miraculous as what it does authorize, but perhaps above all is that it is a self-established government.

Self-government is the foundation of true liberty. Since a true republic is the only government that protects liberty, self-government is what preserves a republic. Self-government, often confused with independence, has more than one real implication. The first implication is of oneself, including their moral compass and standard, political beliefs, and what is held as truth. The second implication of self-government is that of a nation, including its moral standard, political views, and what is held as truth. If both implications are true, can the second exist without the first? During a republic, is the government not a reflection of the governed? If the answers to those questions are yes, then who can argue that the laws of a nation are the result of its moral compass and standard of the people?

The Declaration of Independence asserts that government powers are derived from the consent of the governed and that when any government becomes destructive, the governed have the right to alter or replace it. Once the British crown was removed from power over the colonies, the Confederate American government was fully installed in its place. The post-Revolutionary US lumbered on with a loose union from 1883 to 1889, when the Constitution was finally ratified. The time from the Revolution to Federalization was riddled with calamity and poverty, proving that a decentralized, overly democratic union wasn't working and needed to be replaced.

Upon becoming a constitutional republic in 1889, the best opportunity for a nation to have lasting national prosperity was born. However, opportunity is not a guarantee, and the founders knew that. They also knew that the idea that democracy is the ultimate form of government and that any nation should strive to achieve it could pose a significant threat to the now-installed republic. Democracy was seen as something that appealed to human nature and was renounced through constitutional ratification because the very purpose of the Convention was to install a responsibility-based government, also known as a republic.

Keeping a republic means keeping the Constitution of the United States. Keeping the Constitution, by and large, means first understanding, then obeying it. Washington declared in his farewell speech:

> "Respect for its [The Constitution's] authority, compliance with its laws, acquiescence in its measures, are duties enjoined by the fundamental maxims of true liberty. The basis of our political systems is the right of the people to

> make and alter their constitutions of government. But
> the Constitution, which at any time exists, until changed
> by an explicit and authentic act of the whole people, is
> sacredly obligatory upon all. The very idea of the power
> and the right of the people to establish government
> presupposes the duty of every individual to obey the
> established government."[17]

Clearly, Washington was saying that *having* a self-established government [the Constitution] is wholly contingent on *obeying* the self-established government [the Constitution]. The principle of *obedience* to government is the bedrock of republicanism. Democracy, the government of human nature, is the other way around. Human nature thinks the government should obey the people, thereby running on the *people's will, which is governed by opinion.* Republicanism runs on principle and requires a sense of duty from all. Duty is a function of self-government. Self-government is the government of self.

Employing education, the experience of England's tyranny, and the tenuous Confederacy, the framers were painfully careful to write the Constitution so that every American *could* obey it. Therefore, the wording of the Constitution puts its very existence into the hands of every individual American. Bluntly put, the level of the *sense of duty* of each American is the deciding factor in the *level of protection of actual liberty* for the collective citizens of the United States.

The Bill of Rights was a contested issue among the framers, and fears of future misinterpretation must have been a prevailing fear of the ones who argued against the addition of the guaranteed protections. After all, the main objective of the Constitutional Convention was to establish a republic not easily lost to a rights-based democracy.

Jefferson, a proponent of specific guarantees, said in his second inaugural speech, "During this course of administration, and to disturb it, the artillery of the press has been leveled against us, charged with whatsoever its licentiousness could devise or dare. These abuses of an institution so important to freedom and science are deeply to be regretted, inasmuch as they tend to lessen its usefulness and to sap its safety."[18]

Without a doubt, Jefferson believed the press was abusing guaranteed freedoms of speech and press, thereby putting them in jeopardy. The second term president goes on to use the words *defamation* and *slander,* then acknowledged waiving his option to prosecute the offenders.

Though Jefferson was the primary target of the attempted character assassinations levied by journalistic factions of the time, he saw that the republic and true liberty were the real victims of the maliciousness. Jefferson also indicates in the address that the informed public had dealt with the rogue press accordingly and would do so again in the future. Whichever abuses were dealt with, it was clear that the principle of "respect the established government," which is essential to American republicanism, was violated by the press. Jefferson's restraint was a continued display of his passion for American republicanism.

This leads us to the Second Amendment. Before diving into the protection of a "right," we must first fully understand a constitutional "duty." Outlined below is a portion of the Constitution's provision and guidance for congressional powers and dealing specifically with *national* defense:

Article 1 Section 8; Clauses 11-16

11-To declare War, grant Letters of Marque and Reprisal, and make Rules concerning Captures on Land and Water;

12-To raise and support Armies, but no Appropriation of Money to that Use shall be for a longer Term than two Years;

13-To provide and maintain a Navy;

14-To make Rules for the Government and Regulation of the land and naval Forces;

15-To provide for calling forth the Militia to execute the Laws of the Union, suppress Insurrections, and repel Invasions;

16-To provide for organizing, arming, and disciplining the Militia, and for governing such

Part of them as may be employed in the Service of the United States, reserving to the States respectively, the Appointment of the Officers, and the Authority of training the Militia according to the discipline prescribed by Congress

In the clauses above, number twelve is the only one that says anything about an army. Its wording is carefully limited to "raise and support" instead of "keep permanently." The twelfth clause is immediately preceded by the power to declare war, which further proves that the framers [authors] of the constitution intended for standing armies to be temporary and exist only in times of war and particular need. Although having a permanent army was necessary, the intent was to keep its size limited. With a two-year limitation on funding, the government must review the status of national defense needs and then provide for them accordingly. Paying close attention, it's not difficult to see the intent of the Constitution to limit the size of the Army.

Militias were not only a congressional responsibility, but the framers also constituted executive powers over the wartime militia as well, as you can see in the text below from the Constitution:

Article II; Section 2

The President shall be the Commander in Chief of the Army and Navy of the United States and of the **Militia of the several States, when called into the actual Service of the United States**

Twice in the body of the Constitution, before the "Bill of Rights," the Constitution mandates a heavy reliance on an organized, armed, and disciplined militia, with officers, for national defense. First, the Constitution requires a disciplined militia and prescribes what it is for. Then the clause authorizes training and makes provisions for organizing with various levels of rank, including officers. Finally, militias are made a resource for presidents to mobilize and engage after specifying congressional powers.

The Second Amendment, AKA, the "right to bear arms," starts with the third mention of constitutional *duty* before briefly mentioning a right. With careful attention to the written order of the amendment, let's examine it in its entirety:

Constitutional Amendment II

A well-regulated militia, being necessary to the security of a free state, the right of the people to keep and to bear arms, shall not be infringed.

In the Second Amendment, the "well-regulated militia" part comes before the "rights" part. It goes so far as to delineate the responsibility of the militia as being *necessary* to the security of a free state. It can easily be understood to mean that if there is no organized militia, there will be no security or even no free state. Another way to interpret 2nd Amendment wording is that defending the nation is not in gun ownership or an extravagant military, but lies primarily in the congressional and state duty of maintaining a well-regulated militia.

Two words in the Second Amendment that get overlooked are *well-regulated*. As anyone who has been in the military can tell you, *well-regulated* means organized with a specified structure, including a chain of command, regulations, role-calls and musters, managed inventory and supply, consistent and adaptable training, and physical standards for the members, and closely monitored by authority. The truth is that the "well regulated" part of the Second Amendment reinforces what is already in the Constitution under Article I Section 8 Clause 16 illustrated earlier in this chapter.

The next question that may need to be asked is who will be the militia members? This can be partially answered by referring to the portion of Washington's farewell address above, specifically, "sacredly obligatory upon all."[19] But who is *all*? Thirteen years before his farewell address, General Washington gave his opinion on how to set up the nation's defense and that a small portion should be standing regular forces. Still, the majority of protection should be militia. The militia who and how from General George Washington near the end of the Revolutionary War is quoted below:

> "It may be laid down as a **primary position,** and **the basis of our system**, that **every Citizen who enjoys the protection of a free Government, owes not only a proportion of his property, but even of his personal services to the defence of it**, and consequently that the Citizens of America (with a few legal and official exceptions) **from 18 to 50 Years of Age should be borne on the Militia Rolls, provided with uniform Arms,** and so far **accustomed to the use of them,** that the Total strength of the Country **might be called forth at a Short Notice on any very interesting Emergency,** for these purposes **they ought to be duly organized into Commands of the same formation**"[20]

The concept of having a militia as the basis of uninformed national defense was not concocted from thin air or pious philosophical debate. A common thread throughout the founders was that large standing armies threatened republican liberty, and not so much that they may use coercive force on the people but because they will tend to suffocate the nation of its resources and treasury. History has proven, and it is being repeated, that large armies were financially oppressive and tended to promote entanglements seemingly to justify themselves. At the time, Britain was a primary example of having an overgrown military. The oversized British force was one borne of scraping to maintain its expansionist tendencies.

As counterintuitive as it may seem, neither did George Washington support a large army nor was the outside world any less threatening in his time than it is now. Also, at that time, the realization of overgrown military oppressiveness was as apparent as the effectiveness of militias. One example then is mentioned by General Washington in 1783 while making a case for a militia and against an army:

> "Then passing by the mercenary armies, which have at one time or another subverted the liberties of all-most all the countries they have been raised to defend, we might see, with admiration, **the freedom and independence of Switzerland supported for centuries, in the midst of powerful and jealous neighbours, by means of a hardy and well-organized militia**"[21]

Even today, Switzerland, an example of a militia-based defense, has successfully kept its free government through self-governance, a mutual sense of duty, and obedience to its established government. Switzerland's militia-based national defense standard is what these parts of the Constitution, including the Second Amendment, were all about.

The above discussion of the First and Second Amendments is presented to clarify the differences between rights-based and then duty-based thinking, but also for an opportunity to illustrate three little-known rules about republics or self-established governments:

> ➢ **The Constitution is the highest authority in the land and must be upheld as such.**
> ➢ **The citizenry, and the government, are responsible for holding each other accountable to the Constitution and the founding principles; the republic's security is contingent upon this.**
> ➢ **If the Constitution is undone, then the republic is undone. The loss of moral virtue, lack of accountability, and a lack of being informed precede the undoing of the Constitution.**

Being a real republic means that the Constitution, interpreted through founding principles, is one of the three major components of a self-established government. The other two-thirds of a republic are the people in government and the governed. These three parts are the natural checks and balances of a free government. The checks and balances of a republic are the people checking the government against the Constitution and the founding principles and the government checking the people against the same Constitution and founding principles.

The Constitution is the manual on how the country runs, and the founding principles are how it should be interpreted when referred to. If the people or the government deviate from the Constitution's authority and no accountability is imposed, then more disobedience will ensue. That means that once the Constitution is violated and corrections are not made, it will eventually be like there is no Constitution.

Republics are about responsibility at the core, and failing to carry out the duties of the Constitution results in the loss of liberty and rights. An example is a constitutional mandate for militias discussed previously in this chapter. The Constitution is blindingly clear about the responsibility of Congress and citizens to have an organized and trained militia. However, the Second Amendment is under fire and hotly contested because it gets its energy solely from Article 1 Section 8; Clauses 15-16, and our obedience to it. Therefore, the endangerment of the Second Amendment is no coincidence; it is the reality of a republican-type government. Defer responsibility, and liberty will recede proportionately.

I pledge allegiance to the flag of the United States of America, and to the republic for which it stands, **one nation, under God, with liberty and *justice* for all.**

CHAPTER 3

The Mandate for Morality

"Our Constitution was made only for a moral and religious people. It is wholly inadequate to the government of any other."

—**John Adams**[22]

Until you get to the end of this sentence, you probably never thought that the word *freedom* is likely the world champion of being misunderstood. With all of the science and philosophy employed today, it is unlikely that any person can fully understand the vastness of the word freedom. Though vast, the concept of freedom is still so simple, which doesn't make it any easier to grasp. The word *freedom* has become synonymous with the word *rights* and is frequently used as the focal point in almost every aspect of American culture. It is used regularly as a political sales tool, political stick, political fundraiser, and a justification for obscene military spending.

The word freedom is neither in the Declaration of Independence nor the body of the US Constitution. It appears once in all of the amendments and a mere eight times in all of the Federalist Papers. According to the Declaration of Independence, the self-evident truth is that we have unalienable rights from our Creator: life, liberty, and the pursuit of happiness. Freedom is not listed as one of those rights. Why is that? Well, because freedom is both a gift and a responsibility from God, not a right. It cannot be taken but only surrendered.

In the Virginia Statute for Religious Freedom, Thomas Jefferson stated, "Whereas, Almighty God hath created the mind free," and then brilliantly makes the case that coercing into believing a certain way is merely a practice of tyranny, causing false belief and false religions.[23] The statute's intention, and religious freedom in general, was to restrict the government from assuming responsibility for public religious belief. The question now is, with whom would the burden of belief lie? Could it be anyone but the individual?

Within an individual's life there exist the physical and psychological realms, and that is where freedom either exists or is hampered by bondage. The *Oxford English Dictionary* defines freedom as the power or right to act, speak, or think as one wants without hindrance or restraint. *Act* and *speak* are parts of the physical realm of life that are either with or without limitation.[24] The subject of physical freedom is complex and broad, but examples of general hindrances are; injury, sickness, physical restraints that restrict movement or function, laws that prohibit certain acts or speech, and fear of consequences of certain acts, to name a few. Consequently, outside of physical restraint, injury, or both, actions and words are an expression of the overall psychology of an individual.

A quick example of surrendering individual freedom can be found in something as simple as eating a donut. If you have never eaten a donut and avoid sweets, there is a chance that you have little desire for a donut. Once you take the plunge and try one...or three, you now know why people buy them. The new knowledge now coexists with the incumbent knowledge that no one should eat them.

Now, if you again give in to this new temptation, the health consciousness starts to subside, giving way to the third stop at the bakery, possibly to a habit or bondage. Even as the pattern is being executed, conflicting thoughts exist, but the indulgence continues. Previously, this temporary pleasure did not affect your life, but now it is a *hindrance*. Individual freedom has now been surrendered. Now that the psychology has been altered through taste buds, sweets will pose a new level of temptation by subduing the consciousness of the known consequences. The longer the indulgences continue, the harder it is to stop them. In other words, the longer the bondage goes on, the tighter the bondage gets. This new bondage is there not only by choice but also by invitation.

As with any unholy appetite, there is the inevitable war against the flesh, whether or not physically acted on. War itself, whether psychological or physical, is an invited tyrant like any other form of tyranny.

Believing a lie, however subtle that lie may be, is the cause of bondage. That is why absolute freedom exists only in truth. Truth lives itself out every day before our very eyes. In the previous donut story, the subduing of consciousness away from a known biological fact caused a person to willingly and knowingly risk painful and debilitating diseases. Many examples can be used to illuminate how we surrender our freedom in any area of life. The donut story may seem inconsequential because it is so relatable, but in reality, the fall of nations always starts with these subtle failures of individual self-government.

Truth and consequences are not exclusive to an individual's life but also part of the life of a nation. Paul exclaims in Romans 6:23 of the Bible, "For the wages of sin is death, but the gift of God is eternal life in Christ Jesus our Lord," which means sin brings wrath, and repentance from sin brings life. The scripture applies to humanity, societies, and particularly to nations. The unrepentant sin of a person can be punished on earth and in eternity, but countries can only be punished or rewarded on earth. That means that the wages of national sin are paid in the proverbial present. This was made blindingly clear in the 1860s with the Civil War. As soon as the Constitution was ratified, the United States was marching toward judgment for its immoral conduct of slavery. Although the alternative was no country at all, and many strived to abolish slavery even before the Revolution, it was still national immorality carried by our nation. The fact that it eventually took place in the South only and was inherited from the previous British rule does not change the fact that it was a federal United States problem.

The reality of bondage is that the longer it goes on, the harder it is to throw off. Like any societal immorality or any individual's stronghold, slavery gains dominance in four stages; shameful, accepted, protected, and then eventually enforced. Immorality always starts as shameful and embarrassing, but when the shame of a perversion is diminished, it becomes "socially acceptable." Acceptance of a perversion will uncage it, and once it is out, it begins its campaign of ruin.

King George III struck down anti-slavery laws in colonial America (Barton 16).[25] Once America became a constitutional republic and kept the issue legal, it was nationally accepting slavery. Though allowing slave states into the union at constitutional re-formation was necessary for various reasons and was opposed by many, slavery was still officially accepted nationally (Barton).[26]

It's not far-fetched that people in the South believed slavery was necessary for their livelihood. Laws in slave states were designed to perpetuate the practice of slavery, thereby protecting the conduct as a *protected right*. Laws in Virginia, for instance, enforced the rule by making it virtually impossible to release those deemed enslaved people (Barton 16).[27]

For the more common Southerners, secession was about preserving their way of life, or so they had come to believe, but for the powerful and wealthy, it was more about capital. It is not hard to figure out that the elite class in the South was the primary support for the politicians who legislated in favor of the institution of slavery. If nothing else, the industry of slavery should serve as a lesson for the level of destruction that a concentration of economic power in the hands of a few can have on society. Looking back, one can hardly imagine how such an abomination as slavery was practiced, but that's the depravity of an enslaved mind.

The payment for immorality is bondage or death. In the case of the Civil War, the price was paid with interest. The commonly misrepresented and taken-out-of-context quote "war is hell" is attributed to the famed General William T. Sherman (O'Connell).[28] It's possible that even he did not realize how true the statement was until the brutality of the Civil War began to take the stage. Fought mainly in the South, the Civil War not only far exceeded expectations of gruesomeness but pushed beyond imagination. The wholesale carnage and violence had often been displayed in plain view of the public. The war amounted to a perfect storm of death with rampant disease and frequent battles producing combat death tolls in the tens of thousands. Medical science had not adopted antiseptic practices, while at the same time, new generations of weapons appeared on the battlefield.[29] The Battle of Shiloh, the first mass casualty battle, ended with over 23,000 bodies strewn with moans of severe pain and cries for help. The scene was so astonishingly brutal that Sherman himself was taken aback by the sight of it. This was the first mass casualty battle of the war and alone took nearly as many American lives as the 25,000 sacrificed in the Revolutionary War.[30]

The Battle of Gettysburg was the deadliest of all the war and had taken some 51,000 lives.[31] The war accounted for the deaths of 620,000 military-age American men. The Civil War produced a staggering 49% of deaths from all the battles fought by the United States, including the Korean and Vietnamese conflicts. The number of combatants killed during the four years of Civil War equaled 2% of the American population at that time. It would mean more than 6,000,000 American fatalities if it occurred today (Faust).[32] With the rate and magnitude of death and destruction of the Civil War, it could be described as close to a "national crucifixion" as it gets.

During the Roman Empire, crucifixion was used to show the public what crimes would bring to those who perpetrated them, thereby intending to manipulate minds into submission. However, today it represents hope for humanity. Many pictures of truth can be taken from Christ on the cross. One example is a snapshot of hell, and another is what unrepentant sin does to us physically and spiritually. Through his strategic genius, General Sherman took the war from the conventional battlefield and into the minds of the South. The *March to the Sea,* where Sherman and *the boys* cut a swath of destruction through Southern states, was designed to insight fear in the mind of individual confederates. It served brilliantly as a clencher (O'Connell).[33] The previous monstrosity of attrition was the US's carrying of the cross. At the same time, the capital ruin incurred by the South during Sherman's scourging was the proverbial nailing of the rebellion to it.

The cruelty of the cross is a fraction of a morsel of what unrepentant immorality brings to both man and nations. As cruel as it was, the Civil

War pales in comparison to what was in store for what is now the United States had secession been allowed.

The embedded belief that the industry and the use of slavery were (a) right in the individual's mind is called a *stronghold*. When a believed lie becomes a stronghold, it is in the subconscious mind and expresses itself by overriding the conscious decision-making function of the brain. The longer the bondage remains, the harder it is to break as it becomes more of an individual and a societal norm. The perversion becomes protected by justifying or hiding it, depending on how socially acceptable *it* is. In society, when there is mass acceptance of anything, it tends to become a *protected right*. Once immorality becomes a protected right, its acceptance of it becomes enforced on the whole society in which it exists. Then, once protected and enforced, corruption grows like cancer within civilization and could cause eventual collapse unless stopped. Slavery was immorality that made its way into legality. Like any chronic immorality, the immoral becomes the victim when outside moral forces seek to stop it.

In a representative republic, man can oppress himself because republicanism implies *self-government*. Tyranny is the act of one imposing their view of a perfect world on others, and tyranny starts with respective strongholds. Despotism, defined as exercising absolute power, especially cruelly or oppressively,[34] begins with the *self-oppression* brought on by individual opinion. **To put it bluntly, subjects make tyrants, not the other way around.**

For injustice to take hold, truth must first be broken down. In an individual's mind, when accepting falsities fractures reality's foundation, the thought pattern becomes more and more opinion based. "Opinion" is a view or judgment (perception) formed about something, not necessarily based on knowledge or fact.[35] The point is that in the realm of politics, morals, and self-government, opinion is generally baseless; that means foundationless.

The opinionated or baseless mind begins to govern itself from opinion, becoming weak and more susceptible to manipulation. If a society is easy to manipulate because of its rooting in opinion, then those ambitious for power need only to garner the favor of *public opinion*. The tyrant who comes to power is usually considered the savior, not a tyrant. The despot oppressor derives power from the oppressed by upholding what the oppressed worship and the object of worship is often rooted in the majority opinion. **This is how the institution of slavery continued before and during the Civil War, not because Southerners worshipped slavery, but because they were governed by lifestyle-formed opinions and not virtue or a sound moral principle.**

The first paragraph of the Declaration of Independence contains the statement "...among the powers of the earth, the separate and equal Station to which the Laws of Nature and of Nature's God entitle them...," which indicates the Revolutionary generations lived in a theonomous culture. A theonomous culture is one where as a rule, not the exception, the laws of nature are understood and respected as being established by an overruling God. Generally speaking, during the Revolution, private citizens and public servants derived their moral constitutions from God's laws.

The Declaration of Independence declares that a theonomous culture is necessary for self-governance. "Endowed by their Creator" is as much an enlistment as a deliverer and implies that a set of fixed and familiar precepts must be adhered to for any society to thrive. Self-government is theonomous, and only theonomous cultures are truly self-governed. The Declaration of Independence was written to a tyrant who ruled an expanding empire where a few elites dictated their subject's morals and from where their subject's morals were derived.

The Revolutionary generation lived in a theonomous culture, which means they understood and respected the laws of nature and knew them as the laws of God. They also knew that morality was being lawful, orderly, and respectful of each other. The government was not perfect then, but it was a moral government. Self-government is a society and a government where governing self from an ethical foundation is the rule, not the exception, and that's why the American republic was founded the way it was.

PART 2

Doctrines of Death

The Triangle of DEATHOCRACY

HUMANISM
(often confused with "humanity" but quite the opposite)

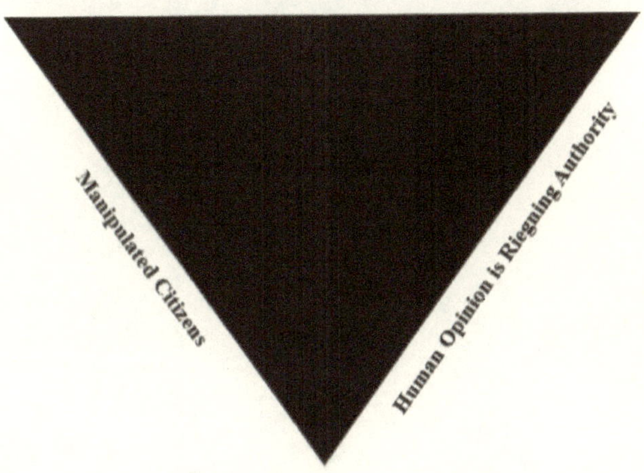

The First Stage of F E A R

False

Evidence

Appearing

Real

CHAPTER 4

The Making of Monsters

"How strangely will the Tools of a Tyrant pervert the plain Meaning of Words!"

—**Samuel Adams**[36]

In the Garden of Eden, the ultimate and simplest form of tyranny was unveiled. God in Genesis 2:17, for Adam's sake, told him that if he ate from the tree of the knowledge of good and evil, he "shall surely *die.*" Later, in Genesis 3, the serpent perverted what God said with "you will not surely *die.*" So, Adam and Eve ate the apple and died the way God said they would because they believed a lie. This is the story of surrendering freedom. They believed a split tongue, a cunning, slithering creature that wanted nothing more than death and destruction, all based on the perversion of one word; *die.* Sound familiar?

Now, for anything to walk, it needs legs. For anything to stand firm, it needs a solid foundation. If any concrete foundation is cracked and never repaired, the crack not only grows but multiplies. The foundation of a nation is no different, and the United States is no different from any other in that regard, past or present.

The foundation of the United States is often thought to be in the Declaration of Independence and the Constitution, but that is only partially true; the Constitution is how our established government is to be organized and protected. The Declaration of Independence is a citation of truth about self-government and serves as a literation of the American mind. Generally speaking, the real foundation of this country is made up of founding principles, the established government (i.e., the

Constitution, laws, and the people in government), and the people of the United States (i.e., society, culture, morals, and industry).

The word "founders" implies people who laid the "foundation" of something. To say "people" is to imply things like moral character, religious beliefs, and political beliefs among other things. In the case of the United States, the founders are those who embedded their moral convictions and principles into the foundation of the United States. If the moral character of the founders is shown to be corrupted, especially the most prominent founders, then that causes cracks in the foundation of the country.

As recorded in the Christian Bible, strategies against the righteous government where drawn up and implemented long ago. The story from Genesis at the beginning of this chapter is a simple example of good government being corrupted through failed self-government. The crucifixion of Christ was not only an example of democracy in action but also of the power of controlling the narrative. The mob that angrily voted for Jesus to be crucified and yet released the known criminal was blind with opinion. At that time, the Jewish elite had established the consensus that Jesus was treasonous. This was done to protect their power, which was at stake with Him being alive—or so they thought. The ones who jeered and spat on Christ when He carried the cross were not only blind to the truth but were also in bondage because they surrendered their freedom to perversion. The Pharisees technically had won a political battle called the *battle of the narrative*.

The rise of political parties that took place in the first presidencies of the US required support, and the *spirit of party* came with that support. Thomas Jefferson's mention of the abuses of the press in his second inaugural speech indicates that the battlefield of the political narrative was alive as far back as revolutionary America.[37] Although historical, today's narrative is a game of power more than ever. It is also more dangerous than ever before, mainly because it has found its way into every aspect of American society and government; controlling the narrative is a politically correct term for *manipulating opinion*.

Partial truths, which comprise the lion's share of what the media produces today, are the most dangerous of lies and the most effective forms of manipulation. Weaponized partial truths are presented with carefully chosen facts, often in the wrong order, to manipulate opinion. The hidden danger in partial truth is that the perpetrator is rarely found to be a liar, particularly in the case of character assassination. In many cases, especially within a culture of lies, the presenter often doesn't think they are lying. To them, it's not lying because they are presenting facts.

Like many movie scripts, false narratives are carefully crafted to have the desired effect on the viewer's mind. In a divisive political climate, scripted narratives become a form of entertainment drama where the target character is painted in the minds of the viewing audience. Television, movies, and televised news media alone account for enough of the tainted stories to make up what can be likened to an *ocean of misinformation*. Most of that ocean is made of partial truth and slanted speech to garner continued support for a belief, partly to instigate an argument. Add social media, blogs, radio, internet media, and all the likes of such to the mix, and there exists nothing short of an onslaught of misinformation and mass manipulation.

The slander of President Jefferson's character is an example of the written witchery not only of his time but of our time as well. You would be hard-pressed to find a modern piece on Thomas Jefferson with a lack of unfounded and discrediting jargon. Today, Thomas Jefferson is casually known as a sort of godless genius philanderer who sought to secularize the government. Among other vile slanders, Jefferson has been baselessly labeled as a secularist who held deistic and humanistic beliefs, a hypocrite on slavery, a malicious editor of the Bible, and an anti-cleric. Most of these mischaracterizations are aggressively promoted in the modern press even today.

Deists believe there is a supreme Creator and that it exacts no intervention in the dealings of its creation. The label of deism has been vaguely painted over the group of American founders, especially Thomas Jefferson. Where the case for deism isn't used in the pursuit of dismantling, then the accusation of *secularism* is the alternate slander used to defame Jefferson. Virginia's Statute for Freedom of Religion, one of Jefferson's prized works, and his belief that man's religious beliefs are not to be coerced by the government are the usual evidence presented in the case to de-Christianize Thomas Jefferson. Furthermore, the evidence used to cause disillusionment often comes from partial and out-of-context quotes and writings. **The followers of this madness do not even realize that they neither have a right to judge Jefferson's salvation nor are they aware that they are merely tearing down their own country by repeating baseless opinions.**

"The hand of providence" was a common term used when Christians of that time explained how they had been protected in times of peril or a great challenge had been overcome. If Thomas Jefferson was a deist who believed in a God who doesn't intervene in the affairs of men, then why would he offer supplications to the God of the Bible in his second inaugural speech as illustrated in the following?

> "I shall need, too, the favor of that Being in whose hands we are, who led our fathers, as Israel of old, from their native land and planted them in a country flowing with all the necessaries and comforts of life; who has covered our infancy with His providence and our riper years with His wisdom and power, and to whose goodness I ask you to join in supplications with me that He will so enlighten the minds of your servants, guide their councils, and prosper their measures that whatsoever they do shall result in your good, and shall secure to you the peace, friendship, and approbation of all nations."[38]

Although this is just one of many pieces of evidence to confirm the founder's beliefs in the Bible and its principles, subversion of this truth has become the rule in American culture, not the exception. Regardless of the soundness of our founding principles, if American society thinks they were laid by deists, then they become perceived as a matter of opinion. Once the American founding principles became subject to consensus, the Constitution and the established government became about man's opinions. Let's not forget that when the government is by opinion, it is really by human nature, which is humanism. **Let us also remember that if our liberties come from man, then they can be taken by men.**

In the world of deism and humanism, all things, whether created or evolved, are subject only to the protection and power of man. In deism and humanism, all power is vested in the opinions of the majority, and the majority decides what is right and what is wrong, not an overruling God. In the end, labeling founders as deniers of the biblical God has created the illusion that the American republic was established on arguable grounds. Then, as a result, society marches along, convinced that there are no consequences for evil. More importantly, this same society unaware of the promise of justice, also thinks that it decides what is moral and immoral.

With moral virtue and the guiding principles evaporated out of American society, the beast of deception is out on campaign like an overwhelming conquering army. In the case of American society, the army of darkness has been on the march for several decades and is now getting stronger by the month, all under the flag of *humanity*. Humanity makes an excellent cover for humanism.

The *culture of sensuality*, often confused with *freedom of expression*, is another significant milestone for the modern self-perpetuating system of deception. Though sexual freedom has proven destructive throughout history, it continues to dominate the scenery of American life with the taboo of the recent past.

Sexualizing a society, which is accomplished by subduing minds from known natural truths, not only puts the masses into various forms of bondage, but more importantly, it escalates into much darker and deeper perversions. Initially, bondage sells products and manifests a culture of human objectification, producing problems like sex trafficking. The skin culture makes the skin profiteers wealthy and opens the door for a whole new world of human ensnarement.

Marketing professionals, who are well trained in psychology, have become highly proficient at arresting and keeping attention. Sex, sexiness, and sexual liberation are now expressed in all forms of entertainment, media, and advertisement due to marketers' progressive utilization. Frighteningly, it is not only in all forms of entertainment, but they also seem to see no limit on the age of the targets.

Currently, simply using explicit imagery to catch the public eye is reserved for the small-timer and amateur as the manipulation industry has moved on to forming demographic groups. Group marketing, as it is called, is the modern and highly effective commercial version of social engineering.

The plan of big brother and big tech was always rooted in collecting data to make behavioral predictions. Still, the information tyrants are more determined to manipulate the belief and behavior of the masses. Group marketing has become an effective behavioral modification system to form lifestyle patterns of the masses. The purposes of mass manipulation vary but generally, some of the main areas targeted are things like buying, voting, eating, general social standing (to perpetuate class and racial tension), and geopolitical views. Group identity, a social engineering practice that directs people's attention to what social group they are a part of or what group needs attention, is one of the main tactics used by marketers. This highly effective mechanism gives them great power over their subjects. In plain view, this *weapon of mass division* has formed its *target* demographics into segments and segments of overlapping elements. Then, marketers craft science-driven material to attract interest from prospective buyer groups that had already been previously type-cast or molded.

For most, the concern is the collection of data, but collecting data is to eventually manipulate thought. As frightening as it sounds, human thought-control is not the end game for the big tech oligarchs. The end game for them is the control of emotions, particularly the emotion of fear.

Sex and other lures of pleasure and entertainment, combined with identity grouping, are the keys to the masses' emotions. Once the emotional gate is open, the marketing investment begins to pay off. Fear, the father of suspicion and division, has always been the critical ingredient for conquerors to gain control of societies. Stalin and

Hitler are two of the most notable fear-driven dictators who exemplify dominating through fear. Horrid madmen are not the only ones who made fear and intimidation their instrument of dominance, but it's also a common tactic in modern warfare, sports, law, and business. The time-tested tactic of fearmongering goes back to the Garden of Eden. There, Adam and Eve were tempted by the serpent with *knowledge of good and evil.* Even though pride was the main thing being appealed to, *fear* of the unknown played a vital role in the failure to obey God's explicit command concerning the forbidden fruit. The *fall* is an example of many things, including the consequences of failing to self-govern by adhering to established truth and then subsequently believing a well-presented lie.

> "Why should I trade one tyrant three thousand miles
> away for three thousand tyrants one mile away?"
> **—Mel Gibson as Captain Martin
> in the movie *The Patriot*[39]**

The fearmongers of today are firmly established in their influence and numbers and spend a lot of resources to incite perpetual fear among the population. The fear machine of today, who ultimately wants control of mass opinion, has the lessons of the past and complete access to the masses through electronics and the internet. The current era is known as the information age. Nearly all people on earth are pummeled with *information* twenty-four hours a day via TV, mobile phones, and computers of various sizes and forms. The assault also employs the weapon of round-the-clock connection of the masses to the masses through social media. This takes the concept of "three-thousand tyrants one mile away" to a new drastic level like three million tyrants one foot away. One thing is for sure about this present scenario, which is that it's a dream come true for those who intend to manipulate and then dominate the thought life of others.

The technology we have today possesses the unlimited potential to enhance our pursuit of happiness and does so in many ways. In reality, the question of happiness is the same as freedom: where does it indeed come from? The answer for both is also the same, and that answer is from the inside. The connection between happiness and protecting freedom may not seem apparent, however, one cannot exist without the other. The chief manipulator, the devil, knows that happiness cannot be stolen any more than freedom can and that it has to be surrendered by the owner. **The devil doesn't just take your joy; he talks you into giving it up and then leaves you with fear and bitterness; more commonly known as worry and spite.**

The foundational principles of the American republic are the primary target of today's army of darkness. Their goal isn't necessarily to steal your happiness or freedom but to control what you think happiness and freedom are. If anyone can own what another believes happiness is, then control can be exercised over beliefs about where it comes from. Then, once the fake source(s) of happiness and freedom is/are fabricated, the fictional sources of health, wealth, and most importantly, moral virtues follow suit. When manipulating these categories of thought happens for domination, the individual is no longer self-governed but governed by opinions from outside sources.

The incitement of fear is the essence of brainwashing. Many examples can be given, but the primary focus of the manipulators is to present and incite the following:

- Fear of supposed evil regimes, terrorism, and authoritarianism to justify an ever-expanding and obscenely large military and intelligence agencies, giving the companies that make military hardware oligarchical power over policy and the treasury.
- Fear of climate change and severe weather to justify an ever-expanding environmental protection regime and obscenely large government entities to enforce unjust and useless environmental laws and international pacts.
- Fear of sickness, insanity, and disability create a chronic over-reliance on medical and drug treatment, which gives a large amount of control over policy and people to big pharma and big medical.

> ➤ Fear of loss of rights and *freedoms* to cause division, the spirit of party, civil disobedience, and the worship of opinion that makes for a weak-minded society, easy to manipulate, and inherently suspicious; which in turn is the platform from which *big tech* stands to control narratives all over the world.
> ➤ Fear of poverty and lack to drive class warfare, and ultimately drive the voting of the coffers and mass dependence upon the government.
> ➤ Fear of discrimination and inequality to further divide, conquer, and ultimately control minds and emotions; in the end, this is **FEAR OF EACH OTHER.**

Although many more examples could be given in this regard, some of which readers may even be thinking of, the truth is that all of the above are direct assaults on the founding principles and the intended republican form of government.

As anger-provoking as this may be, remember that *acceptance* is the first step in becoming a subject and not the other way around.

The Second Stage of F E A R

False

Evidence

Accepted as

Reality

CHAPTER 5

A Perversion's Place

> "The people can not be all, and always, well informed. The part which is wrong will be discontented in proportion to the importance of the facts they misconceive. If they remain quiet under such misconceptions it is a lethargy, the forerunner of death to the public liberty."
> **—Thomas Jefferson**[40]

Fearocracy is a form of government in which fear is levied on its subjects to maintain control. Fear always becomes the choice of tyrants, not only because it's so effective at conquering the mind but also because it is so contagious. Constant worry, a culture of suspicion, and bitter divisiveness are some of the symptoms of a persisting fearocratic society. Once freedom of the mind is surrendered due to a lie being accepted, fear being the trojan that carries the lie, the host mind is now operating from a fear-based opinion. An opinion is generally a baseless perception framed by an accepted lie or false evidence *accepted* as reality.

An opinion-based society is also known as a democracy. Democracy, or mobocracy, is a fictional system of government where power is in the majority. In other words, the opinion of the most significant portion of the masses rules over the minority. According to Plato, republics fall to oligarchy and democracy, then to something far worse (Plato/Jowett).[41]

In an oligarchy, the economic and political power is concentrated in the hands of a few small groups. Oligarchs are often thought of as a handful of select uber-wealthy families or a designated ruling class of elites who are overtly known to be the overruling force of a nation or society. In reality, certain industry elites, ideological movements, foreign or domestic elites, and uber-wealthy elites can qualify as modern oligarchs. Below are the three qualifiers of oligarch status:

1. **Must be considered a rescuer or savior to some degree.**
2. **Must exercise control over a large portion of a citizenry in return for being the rescuer or savior. Then public and private wealth are surrendered, and markets are affected, fabricated, and manipulated.**
3. **Must have obtained enough power to drive the nation's foreign and domestic policies and the country's treasury. This is not to be confused with ongoing political party support.**

For an oligarchy to take the place of a republic, the republic must have its principles forgotten but remain materially and in legality. In essence, the republic is seen as fully functioning for the most part but always seems to have an invisible hand driving it haplessly to self-destruction. The process of the power shift may or may not even be known to the would-be oligarchs since the process of self-government has been broken down so subtly and creating the vacuum for them to exist. The oligarchs become the proverbial saviors as they also have long forgotten the founders' principles. They have only their own experience and nature as the primary source of guidance.

The ultra-opinionated citizenry, overburdened with worry and suspicious of the established government, has unknowingly shifted from principled self-government to partisan self-interest. Since the citizenry is the garden of its leaders, the chambers of the government become the fruit of the populace's embittered roots. Once the oligarchy gets traction, the enlightened are either swayed to the line or separated as rotten and disruptive. The spectacle on display is an expression of the *spirit of party*, a spirit that both invites and is emboldened by the republic's breakdown.

Washington warned of the *spirit of party* in his farewell speech, pointing out the inevitable vengeful factions that would spring forth. Disregarding Washington's warning has brought on undeniable consequences. One of the main consequences is that the American political scene has turned into a freak show of factional malaise. While American society is lost in divisiveness, which parallels the extremes of being opinionated, republicanism is no longer considered a form of government and is relegated to a political party. **Consequently, the Constitution is now merely a talking point that usually takes a backseat to baseless infighting spurred by the latest violation of a right that never actually existed.**

The so-called *two-party system* is thought to be the checks and balances that keep the nation centered. In modern elections, candidates form their political campaigns around holding the party base while gaining a majority of the independent vote. The whole of the legislature and judicial branches are made up of a split between the two parties, and much of what comes out of them is based upon the opinions of the occupying majorities of these branches. The views of the majorities, or the collective opinion of the strongest party, are usually based on what will warrant electoral favor for the party itself, thereby confirming a government *of* and *from* the mob. The election process becomes based on popularity and party lines instead of upholding fundamental American republican principles. The party line, as it's called, is about two things; garnering party support and manipulating public opinion; instead of what is best for the republic.

Again, for an oligarch to be viewed as a savior, there must be a perceived outside threat. Freedom, instead of virtue, becomes the focus, and then the *free* society lives in a perpetual state of threatened freedom and rights. The fear-laden freedom-focused crowd sees the world as either democratic and free or totalitarian and in need of rescue. The *free* countries are considered allies, while the totalitarian governments are thought to need regime change. The non-free countries are considered threats to freedom around the world. In the US, this translates to threats to American national security and its *superpower status.*

The baseless and evil concept of being a *superpower* among the nations in a perceived struggle for global freedom drives a false sense of need for a liberty-crippling military. As the defenders of freedom worldwide, possessing the globally predominant military is considered an absolute necessity.

That predominant military is also an expensive trophy for the protectors of freedom. In today's America, even US presidents are scrutinized for how well they defend freedom globally because America has been convinced that it was appointed the judge and jury of the world's nations. This flawed consensus is very profitable for a few and tragic for many since working Americans pay around half of all they make in taxes to fund the monstrous institutions of global force, surveillance, and medicine.

To solidify the paradigm of the global axis and allies, public opinion must be to despise *non-democratic* world leaders for allegedly oppressing their people. For lack of allegiance to the causes of global freedom (globalism), non-conformant world leaders become the focus of their vilification war chest. With carefully abridged stories, slanted reporting, and out-of-context quotes, foreign leaders who present a contrast in geopolitical ambitions are painted as Stalinistic madmen who must be removed from power. Deploying the usual accusations usually involving some violation of human rights, supporting a terrorist regime, being a dictator, having expansionist ambitions, and a litany of other aspersions are the *de facto* methods of justifying American global serial-meddling.

With a hyper-focus on perceived threats to promote fear of global conflict and inhumanity globally, US military intervention is perceived as a constant *necessity*. The *necessity* becomes the subsequent astronomical spending that is forever justified. With half the globe needing protection from tyranny or invasion, and an axis of evil lurking on virtually every corner of the earth, the instrument of freedom, otherwise known as the US military, sees no limits to its size, budget, or suffocation of American taxpayers. All the while, certain communist and even fully monarchical regimes continue un-contested and even protected by the US military.

Presently, questioning the overgrowth of the US military and imperialistic exploits is off-limits, and any who dare to are subject to accusations of cowardice and supporting fascism. This is an outright fulfillment of George Washington's prophetic warning:

"Excessive partiality for one foreign nation and excessive dislike of another cause those whom they actuate to see danger only on one side and serve to veil and even second the arts of influence on the other. **Real patriots, who may resist the intrigues of the favorite, are liable to become suspected and odious, while its tools and dupes usurp the applause and confidence of the people to surrender their interests."**[42]

—**George Washington**

Before this warning in his farewell address, Washington states, "foreign influence is one of the most baneful foes to republican liberty,"[43] then goes on later in the address to emphasize impartiality and to extend commercial relations while avoiding political ties. This principle is echoed among the founders as non-negotiable in keeping a republic and the true liberty that only a republic can provide. **In other words, attachments become entanglements, entanglements lead to war, and war leads to despair and financial ruin.**

In complete contrast to the founding principle of peace, *commerce, and honest friendship with all countries and entangling alliances with none,*[44] the US-led *global hand of meddling* marches on as if the precept had never existed. While America becomes more divided and bitter, the government and the masses still praise the magnificent power of the US military. This is all while ignoring the extensive damage to the US and the countries in which it meddles.

In one breath, the masses of America rail against being the world police and in the very next breath, declare their vengeful position against the injustices committed by the countries that we are illegally policing. The result is that the military can never be large enough, and no American's prosperity is safe from its egregiousness, except the very, very, very few at the top of the war profiteer hierarchy.

The practice of global policing is not only a chronic violation of the principles noted in the previous paragraphs, but it's also a contradiction to the principles of not having an overgrown military, as delineated by James Madison:

"Of all the enemies to public liberty, war is, perhaps, the most to be dreaded because it comprises and develops the germ of every other. War is the parent of armies; from these proceed debts and taxes, and armies, and debts, and taxes are the known instruments for bringing the many under the domination of the few. In war, too, the discretionary power of the Executive is extended; its influence in dealing out offices, honors, and emoluments is multiplied; and all the means of seducing the minds are added to those of subduing the force of the people. The same malignant aspect in republicanism may be traced in the inequality of fortunes, and the opportunities of fraud, growing out of a state of war, and in the degeneracy of manners and of morals engendered by both. No nation could preserve its freedom in the midst of continual warfare."

—**James Madison**[45]

President Eisenhower also warned about what he called the *military-industrial complex* and how it could dominate national policy.[46] Presently, the term *military-industrial complex (MIC)* is a common part of the English language. Many speculate that it garnishes power through four mediums; news media, the Pentagon and CIA, a portion of the elected federal government (whether they know it or not), and mainstream entertainment (Hollywood). Technically, it would have to be five, and the fifth being the population of the nation the military represents. What is not speculative is that the MIC has the power to incite fear, be the savior, and have a substantial amount of control over US policy and our treasury.

Oligarchies are typically under the control of more than one group of oligarchs. So, has the United States reached that level? John Adams may have unveiled the answer when he warned, "When economic power became concentrated in a few hands, then political power flowed to those possessors and away from the citizens, ultimately resulting in an oligarchy or tyranny."[47] Given what oligarchies and tyrannies are, they can very well be the same; it is hard not to see that President Adams' quote from over two hundred years ago tragically describes present-day America.

Federal policy flowing to the possessors of concentrated economic power can be seen in the marriage between the Food and Drug Administration and the pharmaceutical industry (big pharma). Not only is policy flowing to them and their centralized economic power, but their control over most Americans is alarming. Big pharma's control is exercised in various ways, primarily by garnishing wealth through medical insurance, which often provides policies that allow only for *FDA-approved* pharmaceuticals for treatments. Another way the "medical industrial complex" controls through fear is that many of the masses are driven to prescription drugs to solve many physical and mental ailments, most of which could have been prevented or resolved with no medical intervention.

Coincidentally, many prescriptions are intended to be taken for several years, if not for life. Fear conquers, and sickness and dependency are the keys to the kingdom in the case of big medical. If the masses are convinced that they are either sick, or need something to keep them from getting sick, then the provider of the cure, treatment, or vaccine is now the savior and rescuer. In other words, if people can be made to believe that their health is based on access to a system, then a great deal of liberty has been surrendered to that system. That system now has the ability to expand without limit. It also has the unmitigated power to decide who, and who it does not treat, and that decision is usually based on ability to pay.

Again, the pursuit of happiness is enhanced through the advancement of modern medicine, as it is with technology and its superlatives, but the medical industry has gone far beyond being a resource for the health and well-being of people. Through TV commercials, social media, and news media, the pharmaceutical industry has amassed a frightening amount of control over a population that seems to be receding in physical and mental health. The pharma takeover happened through a complex system of several tentacles, similar to the military-industrial complex.

Although other potential oligarchs are not discussed, one being *big food*, a handmaiden of big pharma, the point remains that America has succumbed to *fearocracy*. As a result of fearocracy taking hold, a dangerous amount of freedom has been surrendered, and the founding principles are forgotten. The process can be summed up as trading in true liberty for the allures of *capitalism* and *democracy*, neither of which are mentioned in the Declaration of Independence or the US Constitution, and both are defended heavily by the majority of Americans. The anti-capitalists defend democracy against the capitalists, and the anti-socialists defend capitalism against the socialists. In most cases, the argument is based on conjecture from both sides, as are the debates about the First and Second Amendments.

The ignorance of history is not as dangerous as the *acceptance* of revised history. If an individual accepts a lie or alteration of history in his conscience, then that individual will be susceptible to believing lies about the present. If a society harbors those lies collectively, it will commit the act of **exercising alternate realities**.

The Third Stage of F E A R

Faithfully

Exercising

Alternate

Realities

CHAPTER 6

The Gravity of National Depravity

> "A general dissolution of principles and manners will more surely overthrow the liberties of America than the whole force of the common enemy. While the people are virtuous, they cannot be subdued; but when once they lose their virtue then will be ready to surrender their liberties to the first external or internal invader."
>
> **—Samuel Adams**[48]

Deathocracy is a condition brought on by a chronic increasing graduation of a society's abandonment of all things that are life and truth. Because a deathocracy results from a persisting *fearocracy*, the same symptoms are shared, only more intense in the deathocracy. Political debate in this climate no longer resembles a contest of ideas but looks more like a steady stream of angry factional infighting. Constant worry shifts to perpetual despair that grows deeper, and hope is snuffed out by the daily barrage of immorality, identity politics, political correctness, fearmongering, and race-baiting. The culture of suspicion spirals into a persisting *guilty first* culture. This climate is particularly harsh to any who endeavor to uphold wholesomeness, constitutional authority, the laws of nature, and of nature's God.

Humanism, now the *de facto* established religion, ushers in the very tyranny the First Amendment was intended to prevent. Under the guise of *faith in humanity*, the self-proclaimed *tzars of what is right and wrong* establish near-total power through their main sects of environmentalism, social justice, secularism, individualism, and intellectualism. As a principal doctrine of operation, humanists exploit the shattered foundation of truth by imposing the burden of guilt and shame. With the "throne of flesh" established, the validity of the Constitution of the United States comes into question regularly, and the only part of it the masses know of are the first five amendments.

In democratic societies, the engine of degeneration consumes the nation's oxygen while fear, guilt, and victimhood are its main mechanical components. The very tyranny caused by the chronic *moral injury* of society also feeds on the same *moral degeneration* that caused it. As the nation's moral fabric unravels, the immoral majority rules over the upstanding few in the name of basic humanity and individual rights. Moreover, since human rights are the focus, anti-humanists are also seen as violators of human rights.

As manners degenerate into nonexistence, all that is anti-civilization is glorified as the pillars of freedom. The population seeks constant entertainment and filters little of what it looks at. Nakedness, suspicion, weirdness, and violence make up most of everyday life. Deathocracy is the goal of the dismantlers and overthrowers, and they desire nothing more than for the masses to be weak-minded and dependent.

Moral injury, a term developed over the last couple of decades, is used predominantly to describe the guilt and shame carried by combat veterans. The condition is brought on by actions, inactions, or experiences that violate their predetermined moral codes and beliefs. The term was was derived from the psychological treatment of war veterans as a differentiator from actual post-traumatic stress disorder.

Many of the men and women who return from serving in the thick of US conflict are burdened with self-condemning thoughts rooted in events that took place during their military tenure. A consequence that can be attributed to this phenomenon is that Americans who previously served in the armed forces (veterans) take their own lives at a rate of around seventeen per day, a rate that is roughly 1.5 times higher than non-veteran suicides. This epidemic has taken approximately seventy-eight thousand former service members' lives from 2005 through 2017.[49]

No less staggering, suicide is the tenth leading cause of death in the

US as of 2019, with over forty-seven thousand suicide deaths that same year. In one day, roughly 130 Americans take their own lives, with an estimated 1.38 million attempts for 2019. The demographic with the highest rate of suicide in this country is middle-aged white men.[50] With these statistics, it would be hard to argue that American society is under some degree of despair. This is just the beginning.

Moral injury is a spiritual wound incurred by a person that, either by itself or compiled with other damages, causes the person to develop particular lifestyle and thought patterns that are either expressions, justifications, or a covering of the wound. Another word for *moral injury* is *pain*. A reality about *moral injury* is that it's been around since the beginning of humanity, seeking to dominate societies. In a close similarity to Germany between the first and second World Wars, moral injury is now the predominant force that drives American politics and culture in the twenty-first century.

Shortly after the First World War, Germany was strangled under hopeless runaway debt caused by losing the war and the reparations they were required to pay. Germans were in great despair and hopelessness (Rickards).[51] This despair and hopelessness fueled the rise of Hitler, a master communicator and manipulator who convinced the Germans that he had the answers. The expansion became part of the answer for Germany to avoid collapse. The build-up and maintenance of a military capacity provided the benefit of production and mass employment by the military and its necessary industrial complex. Conquering other countries was another ploy to avoid collapse because it added outside gains to Germany's failing system (Rickards).[52]

What's essential about the German expansion during WWII is that it is an example of what military expansion indicates about a country. Countries with growing debt, societal despair, and a habit of printing money are in danger of fitting this model. Interestingly, Nazi Germany's immoralities became more entrenched in its culture as they continued. Nazi ideals conquered the minds of Germans more and more over time, and concentration camps were after years of anti-Jewish propaganda. The average

German would have never condoned the Nazi evils, not even the printing of money, had it not been for seeking the unholy savior in the first place.

Having long abandoned the gold standard, the US continues boldly forward with military spending and expansion that rivals any in history, all with no end to any of its conflicts in sight and a seemingly feverish push for engaging in more. The US has forgotten what the military is actually for through repeated and chronic violations of what is moral and foundational. In blatant disregard for the precepts of the founders, the US military now consumes most of the nation's discretionary spending budget. This budget was exceeded in fiscal year 2019 by just under one trillion dollars. Not only does it consume an obscene amount of resources, the majority of its use has been for anything but actual national defense. Minding the world's business, the US military continues to justify its overspending through deliberate mass misinformation and geopolitical hoaxing. *Defense* means defenders of what the *tzars of right and wrong* decide needs to be defended or policed, and that is anything but *national security.*

With a runaway hopeless debt of $28.5 trillion as of July 1, 2021,[53] the US spends over $770 billion on its oversized military, which is more than all the following eleven countries combined. China is a distant second at around $260 billion.[54] The US spends profusely on its military, and we also have a military presence in roughly 40 other countries worldwide. This is what we know of and doesn't include the countries that receive weapons and training. It also doesn't include nations our intelligence services and economic assassins have infiltrated—this is all at our expense and indefensible.

The record military spending likely does not include money and resources sent to countries that can and cannot defend themselves. Many of these countries receive bottomless "aid" from the US Treasury. According to Concern Worldwide USA on *concernusa.org,* "aid" was given to the tune of $47 billion in 2019, with the top ten beneficiary countries receiving 35% of that $47 billion, and almost 60% of that money is allocated for military spending purposes. Those ten countries are listed below as they are on Concern's website *concernusa.org;*[55]

1. **Afghanistan** ($4.89 billion)
2. **Israel** ($3.3 billion)
3. **Jordan** ($1.72 billion)
4. **Egypt** ($1.46 billion)
5. **Iraq** ($960 million)
6. **Ethiopia** ($922 million)
7. **Yemen** ($809 million)
8. **Colombia** ($800 million)
9. **Nigeria** ($793 million)
10. **Lebanon** ($790 million)

Even though the military doesn't officially control empirically where it stands in other countries, the truth remains that it expands continuously…along with America's debt and suicide rate. The overgrown military we were supposed to avoid is now one of America's most significant economic and liberty suppressors. **Because we allowed it, we are now defenseless from it, just as the founders warned.**

According to the National Center for Drug Abuse Statistics, over 70,000 Americans died from a drug overdose in 2019, and roughly 72% of those deaths were from opioid-based narcotics.[56] Overdose deaths are counted as *accidental deaths* by the Centers for Disease Control, a category of statistics that holds a position as the third leading cause of death. Accidental death was behind only heart disease and cancer in 2019. The importance of this statistic will become apparent later in the chapter, but for now, let it be seen as a strong indicator of *deathocracy* in motion.

Americans spent in the neighborhood of $3.8 trillion (Pre-Covid) on medical treatment, including prescription drugs, hospital services, etc.,[57] making the US a distant first in per capita spending among other developed nations.[58] The 2019 (pre-COVID) spending is a 4.6% increase from expenditures in 2018.[59] As cancer and heart disease combined continue to take over 1.2 million lives in the US, the medical industry also continues to grow. As the medical industry continues to expand its dominance in the marketplace, it also serves as an excellent platform to collect the wealth of the masses. This is all while successfully managing to create prescription medicine and medical institution reliance among the American population.

In proper *deathocratic* form, as if the prescription drug industry doesn't confiscate enough of Americans' hard-earned money, the legalization of marijuana is supported by the opinions of 68% of Americans (Brenan).[60] Not only does the carcinogenic mood-altering drug find favor in public opinion, but it is also rising as a perceived medical miracle in thirty-three states and a legal form of recreation in eighteen states in the US.[61] Some states where marijuana is fully legal have experienced all of the effects that illegalization would avoid, according to the National Center for Drug Abuse Statistics, some of which are outlined below:[62,63]

> In Colorado, the cost of legal marijuana to taxpayers exceeds $5.00 for every $1.00 in tax revenue, in addition to expenses such as marijuana-related DUIs that cost $25 million in 2016.[64]

> Suicides where toxicology tests indicated marijuana had been used increased from 7.6% in 2006 to 23% in 2017

> Emergency-room visits related to marijuana increased by 54%, and hospitalizations increased by 101% in 2018

> 19% of teen drivers have reported driving under the influence of marijuana

> Marijuana is the most common illicit drug found in drivers who die in accidents (around 14% of drivers), though often combined with alcohol or other drugs

> Marijuana use that begins at an early age puts individuals at more risk for mental illness.

> Research shows girls (ages fourteen to fifteen) who used marijuana daily were five times more likely to suffer from depression at age twenty-one.

> Daily use in young women is also associated with a significant increase in the chance of reporting a state of depression and anxiety

> 13% of young users will become dependent on the drug.

> ➤ Marijuana can also negatively affect cognitive function, with regular use potentially causing a drop in IQ of up to eight points

The marijuana industry is at approximately $17.9 billion in revenue as of 2020 (Yakowicz),[65] and legalization of marijuana use is promoted with the same veracity as environmentalism. The legalization of recreational marijuana use is now a political line being towed under the guise of *social justice*. Weed profiteers talk up the death agent as if it were never considered dangerous in the face of statistics like 6.9% of twelfth graders use marijuana daily, 43.7% of them have tried marijuana in their lifetime, and 35% of them have consumed marijuana in the last year.[66] Not only that, but 12.7% of children who are twelve to seventeen years of age report using marijuana in the previous year, 5.9% have used LSD, and 778,000 met the requirements of an illicit drug use disorder, according to the National Center for Drug Abuse Statistics.[67]

It should be clear that the $17.9 billion arm of the death industry has harvested its fair share of destruction in the US. It is projected to grow to $50 billion over the next five years with a growth rate of 26%, according to the National Center for Drug Abuse Statistics.[68] **Still, that prediction was before it grew 46% from 2019 to 2020, according to Forbes** (Yakowicz)[69] What will the statistics of suicide, drug overdose, car accidents, and social recklessness look like when this industry is producing five or six times more revenue than it is right now?

It would be foolish to think for a second that *big pharma* isn't working to develop and patent genetically modified marijuana in the same manner that *big food* has with the various plant-grown foods we consume. The *food industry's genetically modified organisms* were developed primarily to withstand Roundup sprayed on the crops. One would have to wonder what superpowers marijuana will possess should it progress into the industrialization phase. It'll also be very interesting to see what mass consumption of marijuana will do for the death statistics after major crops are maintained by spraying pesticides and herbicides on them. From smoking weed, to smoking weed killer.

While reportedly 55 million Americans use marijuana[70] and drug use among eighth graders has increased by 61% between 2016 and 2020,[71] 40 million Americans admit to viewing porn online regularly.[72] Sickening but true, the average age of first exposure to pornography among men in the US is twelve years old,[73] and at the same time (2018), 43% of Americans view porn as morally acceptable (Dugan).[74] Those reporting as democrats, according to Gallup, showed the most significant increase in acceptance.[75]

The US pornography industry revenues are hard to estimate but are safely in the billions (Benes and Ross).[76] In 2019 alone, the world's most popular porn site reported 24 billion visits, and America saw an 11% increase in porn use during the 2020 COVID pandemic (Froubert).[77] In 2013, it was revealed that the US was a distant first in global porn-site web hosting, with 60% of the web hosting to its credit. That means the US hosts more pornography websites than the rest of the world combined.

As the demand for porn increases, sexual human trafficking worldwide expands to one of the fastest-growing crimes in the world. It's not just the volume of porn that grows, but more violent and perverse versions become more frequent. John Foubert's PhD research has proven a strong connection between sexual violence and regular viewing of pornography, meaning the issue is self-perpetuating and causes deeper insanity and depravity.

Pornography is destruction, and its power is growing. Pornography is the essence of human objectification, while women and children are primarily the victims of its horrid practices. More than 50% of those trafficked are for commercial sex, and 71% of those trapped in the industry are women and girls (Brinlee).[78] Not only does pornography generate a modern-day sex-slave industry, but it is also horrifically abusive to the women and girls working as actresses in the porn industry. Since most of the porn users are men, more women and children will become enslaved to feed the growing industry. As more become enslaved, more American men will become addicted to and controlled by pornography and sex addiction. **Just as the slavery of pre-Civil War America**

became more abhorrent simultaneously as it became more prolific, pornography in modern America is doing the same.

However destructive porn may be, the cycle of imperialism, runaway hopeless debt, unholy dependencies, and the several *legislated protections of immorality* add up to a clear sign that the American republic is on its way to a national death. All of it combined ends up being one thing: hopelessness. Some of the key federally legislated protections of immoralities are not mentioned in this chapter but make no mistake, they are in our faces and enforced by the US government; those enforced immoralities (many not said), posing as rights, presents a solid body of evidence that America is facing a high degree of *deathocracy*.

With all considered and hardly arguable, it is incumbent upon the patriot to picture in their mind who will benefit from the continued squandering of America's labor, ingenuity, resources, and the degeneration of our society. In December 2020, the US government was pushing to pass a spending bill that is as economically suffocating to the United States as it is emboldening to American oligarchs. The $2.3 trillion bill proposed for 2021 would send billions of dollars to foreign countries, with much of it earmarked for buying US-made military equipment, US military expansion, the creation of more dependency, useless institutions, and once purposeful institutions made inept by their inefficiencies and wastefulness.

The real tragedy is that every part of the appropriations monstrosity was justified and accepted by one group of regular Americans or another. At the same time, most of the bill will do nothing to promote the general welfare of the United States. The repetitiveness of the fiscal recklessness, especially in the face of the chronic and worsening national hopelessness, is a dead giveaway of where American political power is held; and makes it blindingly obvious what the possessors intend to do with that power. **The only beneficiaries will be domestic and foreign oligarchs who want nothing more from us than our wealth, health, and liberty. We will hand it over to them for at least one more year.**

While grasping mentally the sickliness, addiction, endless wars, loss of liberty, and increasing hopelessness, it's crucial to understand that neither the oligarch beneficiaries nor the government is to blame for two reasons; first, they didn't cause this (subjects make tyrants), and second, *they* won't fix it because that is the job of either enlightened patriots or the despot that comes to power to clean up the anarchical mess that uncorrected democracy inevitably causes. **Another point that needs to be made is that this is *democracy*.**

Democracy is a condition when the unnecessary is considered necessary, and man lives by desire and opinion instead of duty and principle. Oligarchy is when a few control the many and possess state control, but without the label or responsibility of being government. Both democracy and oligarchy lead to ruin because debauchery, excess, and the extremes of wealth and poverty are the products and perpetrators of oligarchy and democracy. Oligarchy and democracy at a point and for a time happen together, while one feeds off the other. Plato said of oligarchies and democracies "that the death of one would be the death of the other" (Plato/Jowett),[79] and according to James Madison, "Democracies have ever been spectacles of turbulence and contention; have ever been found incompatible with personal security or the rights of property; and have, in general, been as short in their lives as they have been violent in their deaths" (Barton).[80] **Unless there is regeneration of the Republic, then once democracy and oligarchy have finally sucked the republic dry through deceitful plunder, democracy and oligarchy will devour each other. That is the violent end of democracy.**

All hope is in the truth and knowing the truth is the critical first step to reversing *deathocracy*. Following are some truths about our nation that everyone must know:

➤ Division alone in the US is deep enough to take down its sovereignty.

➤ The government practices subversion of the Constitution of the United States, and this is a result of the people not knowing the Constitution or the founding principles.

➢ More lies are spoken than truth because most conversations are rooted in baseless opinions (typically from social media).
➢ Immorality is legislated and tolerated regularly; decency and purity are looked upon as oppressive and villainous.
➢ American society suffers from rampant hopelessness.
➢ The published debt of the United States is a severe and real issue, but the apathy towards it is the real issue.
➢ Environmentalism, humanism, and globalism are forced religions, a historically recurring trichotomy of societal ruin.
➢ The United States is engaged in several entanglements globally that do nothing more than enrich oligarchs, create enemies, and squander the future of generations to come.

Open and affirmed subversion of the Constitution and the direct attack on foundational American principles are among the most severe threats to US national security. The divisiveness of state-sponsored fearmongering has inflicted America with political fractionalization to the point that the rest of the world is wondering how we still exist as a nation. If it doesn't stop, and republican order isn't restored, then the following is pretty close to what things will look like:

➢ Dollar velocity could stop, meaning the money will stop changing hands, or it could just turn to absolute zero value. Companies will shut their doors in droves, and no stimulus will help because it will not be able to restore confidence. Confidence is fading at this very moment; much of the treasury has been plundered by COVID stimulus, relief, and vaccines.
➢ State and local governments will become desperate to pay for infrastructure and other obligations. The federal government will be challenged in making retirement and Medicare payments, resulting in tax rate spikes and rapid inflation. Both high taxes and price inflation are methods of wealth confiscation. A visit to a country like Ukraine will be a great lesson of what it's like when a government is broken.

- ➤ 401Ks and savings accounts will be confiscated to pay for government services like infrastructure, police, military, etc. This will be done so that most don't know it's done.
- ➤ Crime will rise due to runaway unemployment, growing poverty, and increased government dependence.
- ➤ The military will be drastically and rapidly downsized; tens of thousands of service members and laid-off Department of Defense workers will pour into an already overburdened economy.
- ➤ Despair will be more profound than the Great Depression of the 1930s, and given what we have seen of recent civil unrest in the US, the level of violence will surpass the crippling despair.
- ➤ What's left of America will be sold off to global central banks and financially dominant countries like China.
- ➤ Countries worldwide will begin to look to Russia and China for increased trade relations as international confidence in the United States wanes.
- ➤ The global balance of power will shift, and foreign countries will treat us as we treated them politically, militarily, and economically.

The above doesn't just describe the path to and the experience of collapse, but it also explains what is happening. When nations collapse, and ours doesn't have to, only the uber-wealthy and ruling elite will escape its remorseless cruelty. That may be because they were so instrumental in plundering that very nation. Unlike the Civil War, surrendering will not end it, and the wrath will push on for longer than four years. The Constitution will likely be completely undone, and the government will be completely restructured. As the mess continues, power will become more centralized, confirming the founders' warnings about democracy turning into tyrannical despotism.

Then, as we plummet further down into despotism, it will get more barbaric. The reality is that it will simply result from chronic individualism, national moral depravity, and the collective abandonment of truth and founding principles. It will be the result of the *four deadly d's*;

#1 degeneracy—This is seen in the education system of the United States as well as in the general public and the US and state governments, and also with elected and appointed officials and employees. If you have doubts about degeneracy happening in America, then take a look at what is legislated from the bench and you will see the legalization and protection of biblical abominations, which are promoted by Congress along with unfettered rights, entitlement and wealth distribution, and more endless wars amid talks of future endless wars and proxy wars. As for the public, compare a pre-Vietnam conflict-era movie to something the average teenager watches now. The list of indicators of degeneracy includes but is not limited to; general manners, percentage of service-age men disqualified for service, the acceptance of various immoralities, etc.

#2 debt—This includes both consumer and national debt. In reality, it is the consumption versus production factor that the masses seem to think will just go away by buying more Chinese products or starting more wars. However, the modern American monetary system is turning the value of its money into zero, which is precisely what happened during the collapse of the Soviet Union and also pre-WWII Germany.

#3 debauchery—This deadly "d" ties into degeneration, but its category is justified. Sin doesn't just apply to cultural sexualization and legislated protections for sexual abominations, but it also implicates other overindulgences of the flesh such as fantasy, over-eating, overemphasis on fitness, over-entertaining, over-medicating, codependency, etc. The pornification, sexualization, and acceptance of illicit drug use in the US alone qualify this category as a quarter of the reasons America is in a nosedive.

#4 democracy—This is likely the biggest of the four deadly "d's" because it is socially and politically glorified. Democracy creates more wounds, drives bitterness, and incites fear and panic while pacifying the masses and numbing them to the oligarchy grift that is wiping them out. Technically, the Bolshevik Revolution was a democracy because it was a mob of mobs in action for *equality*. Republicanism and democracy are not the same, and right now, it is high time to stop thinking they are.

This chapter was tough to write but was necessary. It is the honest look inward to see where we are. You can only fix problems if you know what they are. Furthermore, there is no motivation to fix the problems unless their seriousness is blindingly apparent. Then, if we see the problem and understand and believe the severity, we still fool ourselves if we look anywhere other than the root of the problem to fix it. In the case of the United States, the root is a chronic and increasingly sharper turn from our founding principles and Constitution.

It is often said that if you do anything 10,000 or maybe 15,000 times, you will master it. The truth is that if you do not stick to the fundamentals of whatever you try to master, it will not matter how many times you practice it; you will always be doing it wrong. The state of our country is an example of that fundamental truth. To further that point, you cannot stick to the fundamentals or the *foundation* if you do not know what it is. **This all means that the problems are unknown because the foundation is unknown, and the government is not our government anymore as a result of it.**

PART 3

The Process of Patriotism

Triangle of Recovery

CHAPTER 7

Know Truth

> "The man who reads nothing at all is better educated
> than the man who reads nothing but newspapers."
> —**Thomas Jefferson**[81]

Oxford defines the word principle as "a fundamental truth or proposition that serves as the foundation for a system of belief or behavior or a chain of reasoning."[82] It is also defined as a rule or set of beliefs defining one's behavior, indicating a requirement to have a set of principles to be self-governed. The *Merriam-Webster Dictionary* defines truth as "the body of real things, events, and facts, which is a definition that leaves truth open to 'perception."[83] It may make more sense if the truth is the whole body of real things, all events, and facts, in the correct order, which removes all possibility of blurred truth by *perception*. A blurred truth is a perverted truth and a partial truth taken as truth is a total lie. **Where lies thrive, society dies.**

The *Oxford English Dictionary*'s definition of *principle* starts with "a fundamental truth or proposition," and it needs to be asserted that our founding principles are not propositions but fundamental truths. Knowing truth is *knowing*, not *thinking*, that what our founders intended and set forth as a principle was the way a nation was to conduct business. Dismantlers were working even in the 1770s to find any little crack to stick their divisive claws through, and the founders were well aware of their existence.

The only thing that has evolved since the founding of the US is technology. Now that the devising propagandist no longer needs to hang paper to get to the masses, citizens must be even more in tune with principle and truth to maintain an impermeability to divisive beliefs. This is an unchanging principle of true republicanism, and the closer we get to collapse, the more apparent that truth becomes.

Fear is a contagion but can only spread in an uninformed society. Since fear is a result of a false perception, it is also the consequence of being uninformed. Being uninformed usually happens due to "being in the know," which results from being entertained. Society kills itself by trading in "informed" for "entertained." Engaged communities become fearful and suspicious because they are outwardly focused. An outward focus also means a lack of self-assessment and self-governance, harboring false fearful perceptions, and being easier to manipulate.

Dutifully informed societies are inward-focused and have developed the ability to discern false evidence from the truth. An informed citizenry that knows its Constitution, its founding principles, and the high moral character of its founders is hard to scare, difficult to manipulate, and its government knows it. **A dutifully informed nation has a government that knows better than to lie to its citizenry.**

The word *informed* implies nothing and is very specific. If the American republic is to remain standing, instead of collapsing into chaos, we must stop confusing "in the know" with "informed" and become informed.

There are two categories where American society has failed in its pursuit of truth, justice, and liberty. One is by being deafened to the founded principles of American republicanism, and the other is psychological separation from general reality. As a result, society perceives government as a political gotcha-game drama, and all things meant for entertainment now shape perception. Americans give as much weight to what an actor, football player, or pop star says as they do an elected official, and as a result, elected officials have become a part of a sport or melodrama. This is how our politics have turned into popularity contests; that is democracy.

Theology, history, physical science, foreign policy, and morality are now decided by movies, documentaries, social media, and news pundits supported by their contributors. Need examples? Look no further than what you think about the following: political parties, global politics, specific political figures, the founders, the military and war, health insurance, the economy, patriotism, the Constitution, God, religion, Heaven and Hell, your neighbor, etc. Go back through previous chapters of this book, think about what you disagreed or agreed with or what you saw that may have been surprising, and think about why it conflicted with your current perception. At the very least, there may be an awareness of any divide between your perception and what is actual.

A critical step in becoming informed is understanding that there is very little room for opinion in the government and life in general. Opinions are a product of human nature; that is why it feels so good to give opinions and why opinions are so entertaining. Opinions should be the exception, not the rule. The problem today is that opinions are the rule, and the truth is the exception. Everything today is about opinion and forming opinions. How often have you heard "I can form my own opinion" or "the experts are saying"? How much of news media production is rooted in opinion? Have you noticed that all the guest *experts* on the news shows are there to give an opinion? What about blogs, podcasts, YouTube channels, etc.? How much of it is based on anything foundational? Or at least with the rare exceptions. Have you ever asked what you learn after consuming this form of entertainment? This doesn't mean that we should stop using all of the social media, but can we honestly say that we aren't overrun with it?

Politics, conspiracy theories, and the rumors of war have come to be the meat of entertainment in America. More of us should think about the intent behind the phenomena. It's not just about what information we consume but also about what it is designed to do. It doesn't just insight a feeling; it also invokes a thought pattern.

Virtually nothing is without a plan in this day and age. *The Revenant* (2015) was a great movie, except that it was wrought with anti-American sentiment. You may still be asking what the political agenda was in the movie *The Revenant* (2015), and the answer is that it was the promotion of the idea that America was built on genocide and racism. As the movie portrayed, the US Army brutally killed the main character's Native American wife (or woman). The wife (or woman) could have died from disease or accident, but a negative stigma was promoted when it didn't have to be. The movie was about a man named Hugh Glass, and no one questioned why the Native American wife and son were inserted into the story when there is no evidence of their existence. The movie itself was very entertaining, but the damage is done. Most who have seen the movie do not know that the main character's family, and their tragedy, were added for effect. This is only one movie, and one genre.

On another front, the weather exploitation industry now participates in one of the most divisive fearmongering campaigns to date. Weather service providers work hard to convince the public that the climate is spiraling downward and that the earth is going to be too hot to live on in a few years because of human activity. Major networks and weather service channels make fearmongering TV programs like *2020: The Race to Save The Planet*. In the program's advertising, the democratic party is portrayed as the saviors of the planet. Again, no one questions why these agendas are perpetuated on supposedly non-political media sources, or NGOs.

It's hard to argue that climate change would be more believable if it weren't as political as it was. However, pictures of melting ice, forest fires, and hurricane damage fill our media devices worldwide to scare the wits out of the unsuspecting masses. It is hard to imagine that this campaign isn't for political coercion. It seems to be working very well since you can hardly find anyone with the guts to speak against it. It also looks like the world is behind the fantastic plans of the global elites. If only we could all understand that ice melts on the caps yearly. While one cap is melting, the other is refreezing, so the images of the melting ice are regular at that time of year.

This is all not to say that we shouldn't be careful with the environment; it just means that the political argument only serves to destroy societies. If society did less arguing and fearmongering, we would be further down the road with more efficient uses of energy. This we should be able to get behind.

Consensus, another word for groupthink and mob rule, is the end goal of mass manipulation. Entertainment is likely the most effective form of manipulation because it is so subtle. Hollywood, a puppet for the oligarchs, can actively participate in mass manipulation and then defer the responsibility of truthfulness merely by being *entertainment*, even while openly supporting or attacking specific political figures and parties. This cycle of manipulation is evident in the way legislation follows popular opinion. The news media sheds accountability by reporting factually, but in a way that supports their desired narrative. Both entertainment and news media participate in the current cancel culture, which is the death of the First Amendment. The public tolerating the news and entertainment media's malicious insurrections is equally to blame for the end of the First Amendment.

To be intentional about reviving our Constitution first requires a clear understanding that there is an ever-present force that wants to install prejudice and form perception. The manipulators know that their message works on some groups one way and then another way on others. Manipulated public political consensus is a work of the devil that breeds argument, and argument breeds division. The division is precisely what the dismantlers are after. Even the most well-intentioned who say, "we need to unite on the issues," do not realize that the issues are there because we are not united. This becomes a cycle as focus on issues becomes an argument, and the more ideas, the more divisive we become.

In the same way that you cannot serve two masters because you will love one and hate the other, you cannot be informed and constantly entertained at the same time. To be clear, while constantly entertained, you are serving a master. When you are becoming informed, you are helping your country; while trying to do both, you will knowingly or unknowingly hate one or maybe both. Becoming informed is about leaving the consensus, and to leave the consensus is to put down the constant entertainment. Entertainment includes news media, social media, the general opinion industry like podcasts and blogs (rooted in spite and opinion), and entertainment like TV, video games, etc. It sounds like a violent shift in lifestyle, but once society begins to turn away from the *feed* and the *noise*, we will realize that there is mostly death in the ocean of misinformation. Disconnecting from the garbage pile of the opinion industry will allow patriots to reacquaint themselves with the *pursuit* of happiness. Turning away from the consensus and the manipulators will allow our nation to pull back to substance and principle.

Objectivity, often confused with open-mindedness, is a major building block of liberty. It is where the Sixth Amendment, which guarantees the right to a trial by jury comes from. Objectivity is the antithesis of prejudice, and if you are not objective you will be subjective and subject to manipulation. In seeking truth, one must be intentional in viewing things without the taint of emotion or preference. In other words, to be objective, you must drop the prejudice. Objectivity must be a habit, and good habits require intentionality to form. Objectivity requires loyalty to the truth, and loyalty requires effort. Becoming informed is a process, not a journey, and understanding that the founding principles are simple will make the process much more efficient. Becoming informed is ceasing to be a subject and a victim.

In the pursuit of truth, obsessive objectivity will breed the ability to discern whether you are taking a stand or merely taking sides. Founding father and fourth US President James Madison wrote, "Truth delights in plainness and simplicity, and it is the counterfeit alone that needs ornament and ostentation" (Barton),[84] which means the truth is simple. It also means that the truth with decoration is a lie with camouflage. The truth doesn't need the variation and pretentious dressings portrayed in news media and Hollywood productions. For them, the simple truth is not profitable enough. All generations are tempted to dissolve truth in society. We are no exception. Below are some examples of how the truth has dissipated out of American culture and the damaging effects it has caused.

(Lie) The US is a democracy—The founders were careful to form a republic and were clear that democracy is *deathocracy*. Article IV, Section 4 of the Constitution of the United States reads, "The United States shall guarantee to every State in this Union a republican form of Government..." which implies absolutely nothing about us being a democracy. Democracy is never mentioned in the Constitution of the United States, so technically, becoming a democracy would undo the United States as it was founded. **The field of damage** encompasses such things as the masses voting themselves the coffers while the state and federal governments subsidize the majority of the population. In a self-governed republic, representatives are elected because they are honest God-fearing men that can be trusted with their positions. Had this been the case in the US over the last few decades, the calamities caused by the onset of democracy would have been prevented.

(Lie) The central banking system and a large debt are necessary for national prosperity—Alexander Hamilton clearly stated that the national debt should be kept small. Many founders (more anti-federalists) opposed central banks; Thomas Jefferson thought the system would be more dangerous than standing armies. **The damage** is multifold, with a growing national debt being the primary consequence. Not only does the debt continue to grow, but taxes will grow with it. The apathy toward the public debt, while private debt and subsidies grow, the US continues to practice a paper-based fiscal system instead of the gold standard, which perpetuates the engagement of a global currency war, and quantitative easing to keep the dollar from rollercoaster evaluations. The Federal Reserve is touted as a savior of American economics but is likely the biggest tragedy of all.

(Lie) America's economic system is capitalism—There is a need for capitalism in our economic system. The capitalist-level investors bring much of the value our system possesses and are necessary to our economy and prosperity. However, the constitution does not mention any economic system but implies the free market. The free market, or free enterprise, means that the government doesn't own the companies; the people do. Capitalism is a level of investment within an economic system, but not the system itself. The constitutional intent was to be competitive, provide a healthy selection, and keep prices down. A free-market system is about skill, leadership, apprenticeship, production, and a culture of service, quality, and innovation. Capitalism is about the bottom line and doing whatever it takes to achieve the largest profit available. **The damage** caused has been jobs are outsourced in droves, factories are moved overseas, and products that should be made in the US are imported. Big business in America is the centralization of economic power. While we don't want the government to own the businesses, it's worse when a business owns the government. Theodore Roosevelt pushed the anti-trust laws for a reason: to avoid precisely what we have now. Remember, we have the highest level of debt since post-WW2.

(Lie) The large military preserves our freedom—A large military provides enormous wealth to the military-industrial complex and causes debt. Furthermore, the over-taxation of the citizens is where that wealth comes from. Being moral, unified, industrious, and respectful to other nations is how we should protect our liberties. **The damage** this has caused is as tragic as it is tremendous. The perpetual conflict, the mental and physical anguish of American combat veterans, the moral injury of combat veterans and American society, the monetary expense with no tangible benefit, and the global tensions are just the beginning of what America is going to experience as a result of its overgrown and overstretched military. The chronic and persistent subversion of the Constitution and founding principles from our oversized military cannot be overlooked.

Then there is a growing perception that if we don't maintain a grossly oversized military, something will gobble us up. Furthermore, the large military has brought a feeling of great power to the US; with that power, it has become easy to assert judgment of how foreign governments govern. That judgment is usually based on consensus, primarily by those who support the idea of a large military. A large military equals sizable military spending. It is nothing short of public plunder.

It would be impossible to list all of the examples of how reality and history have been perverted, but the aforementioned is a great place to start. It goes without saying that all nations need some sort of permanent military and banking system, but shouldn't there be a check to them? That question among others can be answered by comparing what is happening now to the principles in Chapter 1 of this book.

If you don't know what is true, then you are limited in countering lies and hopeless in countering *deathocracy*. Knowing the truth is not only patriotic but also the only way you can properly exercise the First Amendment.

CHAPTER 8

Speak Life

"But what comes out of the mouth proceeds from the heart, which defiles a person."
—Jesus Christ, Book of Matthew, 15:18

Our words are powerful enough to either revive or continue destroying our country. What we say even in general chatter is a matter of national security because the security of our sovereignty is purely reliant on the moral character, and honesty, of our society. Becoming informed is knowing the essential truth. Knowing the truth is possessing knowledge of our foundation. Speaking truth indicates understanding converted to wisdom because wisdom is foundational; opinion is baseless.

George Washington said, "Honesty is always the best policy" in his farewell address,[85] and the founders, as a rule, exercised an asserted effort to make telling the truth a habit in their lives (Barton).[86] That means truthfulness is integral to our American foundation. According to the Wallbuilders organization in their book *Ethics: Early American Handbook,* a 1999 rendition of an American moral code textbook from 1842, adding to, taking away from, or repeating what you do not know to be the truth as if it is the truth is lying; even if you only did not correctly verify or were misinformed (Barton).[87]

There are several ways to lie that are not so obvious or even intentional. For example, repeating the lie that Thomas Jefferson had an affair with Sally Hemings comes from unfounded reporting, or not knowing for sure, and the *mistake* of believing the *misinformation*. Regardless of the coercion that preceded the falsity and all the support behind it, it's a lie if it is not valid. An entire book could be written on how the proliferation of this Jefferson lie has fueled the degeneration of American culture, but the real point here is that unless you know something for sure, you are not sure. If you say something you are unsure of, you are likely perpetuating a lie.

Another example is the proliferation of the word *democracy* as a form of government, more tragically, *our* form of government. The word *democracy* is not an innocent buzzword; it's a tool for dismantlers. It is a word that is repeated in a way that defines the United States as something contradictory to what it is supposed to be.

Reversing deconstruction of the American republic will require a tighter talk; or taking the conversation back to the foundation and true American republicanism. **Keeping a tight tongue means sticking to fundamental American principles and the Constitution.** Reigning in what can only be called hyper-gossip will prevent those in this practice from being reduced to mouthpieces for the humanist/globalists and oligarchs.

Abiding in truth means eliminating words that have corrupted our national character and caused deep and chronic division. For example, the terms *conservative* and *liberal* have become so divisive that each has become an industry of its own. While one leans towards traditional values and the other values a more progressive ideology, the argument never goes back to the US Constitution or foundational principles.

The baselessness of the conservative versus liberal vitriol is partially an evolution of the capitalism versus communism struggle of the Cold War era. Somewhere in history, *capitalism* became synonymous with *democracy* and *freedom* and then took over as our form of economics. **Democracy and capitalism together usually wound up as *democratized* wealth. Democratized wealth is socialism.**

Capitalism becomes runaway capitalism. To have *capitalism* as an economic system, instead of a competitive free enterprise (CFE) or a *competitive free market (CFM),* is to have wealth concentrated in the hands of the few eventually, and therefore those few possessing the political power. That is an oligarchy. *CFMs* promote skill and leadership advancement and produce a robust and balanced labor force. *CFMs* put a premium on industry, quality, and efficiency, while capitalism glorifies capital and consumption. *CFMs* and republicanism promote work, wisdom, and wealth creation through a competitive and productive industry. Capitalism (the so-called national system) and democracy become wealth confiscation and redistribution, otherwise known as a nanny state.

Informed patriots understand the founding principles and therefore think differently about the words *democracy* and *capitalism* as identifiers of American society. Capitalism is not a bad thing, but it is not an economic system. To end the condition of doom, we must stop promoting the cause of it. Therefore, the word *capitalism* should be changed to *Competitive Free Market or Competitive Free Enterprise,* and *democracy* should be replaced with **republicanism.**

A large portion of this chapter was spent on using the words capitalism and democracy because of the damage they have caused. The more damage they cause, the more pervasive they become. The more pervasive they become the more divided America gets. The language makes the difference. However, even though this book cannot cover all of the national verbal mishaps and outright destructive phrases, many vital needed corrections are below.

"The US is a hybrid democracy/republic" and a "representative democracy"—Since many modern definitions of democracy include the representation component, it's common for Americans to be convinced that our Constitution and electoral process is a form of democracy. However, the truth is that a nation is either a republic or it isn't. A country is either principle-based and self-governed, or it is opinion-based and headed for despotism. Remember that the US has already been through the representative democracy phase, and all patriots should research this point. Furthermore, true republics, if kept, offer all of the liberties but also require the responsibilities necessary for good government and prolonged happiness. Democracies provide the mere illusion of freedom and incite division. The year 2020 is a case in point in more ways than one.

"The US was built on religious freedom"—The US was founded on republicanism, and the culture it was formed in was theonomous. That means that as a rule, not the exception, God's laws of nature were generally held up as truth culturally. Nature's God was the sovereign authority, judge, and Creator of all things, including nature and man. It is only the theonomous culture of which a republic can survive. It is only a true republic where a nation can have liberty and peace. Democracies are excluded from republican benefits because liberty and peace come from God; democracies rely on the majority opinion while excluding the laws and precepts of a sovereign God as the moral compass. Religious freedom is merely a component of true republicanism.

"This country was built on Judeo/Christian values"—There is nothing "Judeo" about our foundation or principles. The Judeo-Christian presumption is deceptive and divisive, distracting Americans from what the nation intended. Article VI of the Constitution stipulates that no religious test be required for public office. Still, the founders warned about the necessity to elect God-fearing, morally sound men to those offices.

"We are being censored" / "My First Amendment rights are being violated"—The abuse of the First Amendment is its worst enemy. A large majority of social media platforms have tendencies to be biased and manipulative, but they are not the official government (yet). The lifeblood of the First Amendment is truth and principle. Our free speech guarantee was explicitly designed for the citizens' protection while bringing a grievance of government injustice, immorality, and negligent wastefulness. Social media is merely a business, and it is the user base that has empowered big- tech to extend far beyond the commercial realm.

"I support the Second Amendment"—Although infringing on gun ownership rights is a most basic form of tyranny and un-American, this argument continues to be based on the premise of rights. The First and Second Amendments are a tiny part of the Constitution but are often seen as the basis of all that is American. Neither the Second Amendment nor the Constitution needs our support, but it does require our obedience. Article I Section 8 of the Constitution calls for organizing, arming, disciplining, and calling forth a militia. Article II Section 2 defines the president as commander in chief of the army, navy, and the militia of the several states. If it weren't for past and present disregard for the Constitution, there would be no argument over the Bill of Rights. The founders intended that every man should be capable, ready, and equipped to defend the country.

The troops defend/protect freedom—The oath of the military says protect and defend the Constitution of the United States, not freedom. Obeying the Constitution also protects the Constitution, which protects the country. A moral nation is the best-protected one, while an overgrown military defeats its own purpose and drains the land of its liberty and resources. As stated before, there is supposed to be a militia, and that militia is to be our primary form of military posture. Instead of obeying the Constitution and having a natural mechanism to defend our liberty, we are now closer to being defenseless against domestic tyrannies and against the large military we were never supposed to have.

"Western society/Western culture"—America is not a member of the *Western society* club any more than Belgium is a province of Russia. America is American society. Saying that we are a part of Western society implicates us to a philosophical union with European countries. Not only does it entangle us to ideas and traditions of other nations, but it also creates an *against-them* stigma towards countries that are not *Western* or do not adequately meet *Western* government standards. Being *Western* is code for being *global* and a justification for NATO expansion. Saying "Western society" or "Western culture" isn't a problem unless America is lumped into it. It's impossible to be exceptional if you identify as the same as everyone else.

"Leader of the free world" refers to the president of the US—Though America should strive to be exceptional and a leader in virtue, the president of the US is just that and only that...the president of the United States. The title "leader of the free world" really means controller of the world and global judge of who is free and who is not. The president of the United States is the executive of the federal government and the commander in chief of the military and militia when called into service according to the US Constitution; that job alone is hard enough, so let's be okay with what it is.

"It's a free country"—Free countries and democracies are not self-governed republics; they are free-for-alls on their way to anarchy, and then on to cruel despotism. The primary source of freedom in a free country or democracy is man, and the primary source of liberty in a republic is God.

"This country was built on criminality/rebellion" or "Americans are inherently rebellious people"—This contradicts the Declaration of Independence, the Constitution, and the character of our revolutionary generation. When America struggled during the Revolution, it was against a tyrant of tyrants. The struggle for American Independence was undeniably just and confirmed with victory and the most genuine opportunity for a prosperous republic. The United States was built on moral purity and republican principles.

"The flag stands for freedom"—Freedom is nowhere in any accurate description of the symbolism of the American flag because *freedom* is not what it stands for. The "stands for freedom" term undermines what *Ole Glory* represents. The idea of freedom as a national symbol has led to long, expensive, and tragic military entanglements covered by the false umbrella of defending freedom. A genuine description of what the colors and arrangements on the US flag mean, which are generally virtue, resilience, and unity, can be found at colonialflag.com.

"Empires usually last about this long"—It is true that empires fade into oblivion, but the United States doesn't have to. Empires become empires because they get away from their republican principles and constitutions. Republics have no expiration date as long as they stay republics; that's why George Washington warned us in his farewell address.

It's a global economy/society—The truth is that global trade has always existed, and international discourse has always affected national economies. Before America was even discovered, whatever the known world happened to be was economically intertwined. Point and case examples of historic global connection can be found with the silk road, Alexander's conquests, and even the Barbary Pirate Wars. Not only was there an economic connection, but a social connection also existed, for example, King Solomon and Beersheba, the Spartans and the Persians, and the fact that when Jesus was crucified in Israel, Israel was under Roman rule. The Declaration of Independence mentions as a reason for separation from Great Britain that the king "Cut off our trade from all parts of the world." There has never been a time when nations were not tied together economically. However, that doesn't mean that all countries are supposed to be under one global flag. It is evil to suggest such oppression. It also doesn't mean that all nations must be passionate about any cause or form of government. Simply put, no country is obligated to the whims and demands of the globalists or advocates of democracy or be subject to what a few hold up as their view of a perfect world. Globalism means national *deathocracy* because it requires the death of nations for it to thrive.

I believe that.../In my opinion...—Before one gives their opinion or blurts out what they think, especially concerning other Americans, other world leaders, and just in general, it's essential to think about whether they know what they are saying is true. Again, arguments and commentary should be rooted in truth and interpretations of the truth.

Many other terms and speech patterns could be addressed, but with recent events like the 2020 elections, one thing that has come to light is our perceptions of each other. Social media looks more like an ocean of verbal carnage than a communication method. The name social media should be changed to *medium of malice.* The vitriolic slander, tongue lashing, and verbal abuse in e-space and on TV is nothing short of eating ourselves alive. Most of what's said is baseless and results from a *culture of suspicion.*

What we say to each other and about each other serves as more of an indicator of how we view one another. What we say is from what we think, and what we believe is further confirmed by what we say. Speaking truth is speaking life. Speaking life is choosing life.

CHAPTER 9

Go the Way

"Our safety, our liberty, depends upon preserving the Constitution of the United States as our fathers made it inviolate. The people of the United States are the rightful masters of both Congress and the courts, not to overthrow the Constitution, but to overthrow the men who pervert the Constitution."

—Abraham Lincoln[88]

The United States of America is in a more critical time than ever before, which could mean a brighter future than ever imagined. It may seem complicated to understand how it's possible to survive long term, much less have a bright future, but consider that we are the only nation to fight within itself to free its slaves. Yeah, that was us! However, we must first recognize the present condition is not because of China, Russia, or Islamic terrorists. No president, Congress, Supreme Court, or anything else can be directly blamed. Only *we, the people,* which encompasses you and me, and the government we've chosen, are the cause and the solution.

One golden rule to national sovereignty is this; we will stand united, or we will all go down together. That means, united or divided, what happens to us will happen to all of us.

No republic is fail-proof, and if the right choice is not made in short order in this republic of ours, the collapse described in Chapter 6 will continue to the point of no return. All nations are subject to the wrath of God when they go morally rogue, but not all nations have the republican foundation we have. Jesus said in His own words in Luke 12:48 that "everyone to whom much is given, of him, much will be required," and we were given more than all other nations and an abundance of grace. That means we may have a longer rope than other nations, but if we get to the end of that rope, we fall as a nation. We have been assigned a specific duty as an ordained republic to lead the world in how to be a virtuous and happy people and if we fall, it will become someone else's job. Life or deathocracy is a choice. Choosing life means fighting for the republic and its place of honor and leadership for all the world to learn from and emulate.

The world is hungry to see a united and just America, but first, we must experience the peace that unity, order, and the preservation of life would bring. When Americans stop infighting, repeating the lies of the evil one, and begin to move forward as one, other Americans will see it and want to copy it, and our elected leaders and representatives will fear us more than the oligarchs.

The *way* is simple and a loose summary of the founding principles. It is where the cycle of an alternate reality ends. It's called FightFOURLife, and the "FOUR" stands for; forgive-obey-unite-repeat. A breakdown of the FightFOURLife is below.

Forgive

> "Forgiveness does not mean ignoring what has been done or putting a false label on an evil act. It means that the evil act no longer remains a barrier to the relationship. Forgiveness is a catalyst creating the atmosphere necessary for a fresh start and a new beginning."[89]
> **—Martin Luther King, Jr.**

Forgiveness is the cure for the bitterness that has gripped our nation. As discussed in previous chapters, bitterness and fear are the primary control tools for the manipulators and oligarchs. Bitterness and fear are the real robbers of personal freedom but to forgive is to be free, and to be free is a civic duty. Most (if not all) crimes, corruption, debauchery, and immorality can be traced back to a deep-seated spiritual wound within the perpetrator. That means the transgressor is in bondage to the wound or the moral injury.

Evil begets evil, and moral injury begets guilt and fear. Bitterness fuels the propensity to victimhood, and victims are predisposed to fear. The longer a wound goes untreated, the worse it gets. The worse the injury gets, the more medication is needed. The drug comes in the form of sex addiction and pornography, victimhood, and rebellion, to name a few. The more medicine is taken, the more that will be needed, and the more miserable life becomes.

Misery loves company, and it invites by infliction. Unforgiveness burns up its host and inflicts those around them. The unforgiving soul causes moral injury and passes it on to generations. Unforgiveness turns parent against child, child against parent, brother against brother, and fellow citizens against fellow citizens. Bitterness feeds the *spirit of party* and gives partisan manipulators the energy they need to work their divisive plans.

Forgiveness starves the devising wicked of their corrupting power, but forgiving is often aborted for lack of ability to forget. Neither is acceptance nor forgetting required to forgive. No matter how the wound(s) were caused, only *true forgiveness* honestly deals with the injury, and only *true forgiveness* brings true healing. *True healing* is the only place you can find true liberty.

The first person that needs to be forgiven is oneself—the inability to forgive stems primarily from chronic guilt. Guilt is often seen by the person as a mechanism of self-assessment while, in reality, it is an expression of pride and a diversion from dealing with the issue. Letting go of guilt and shame, the primary weapons of deceivers, releases the bonded mind to see the truth. Self-forgiveness, not acceptance, shouldn't be overlooked in genuine forgiveness and should be considered a critical first step.

Confession is essential to forgiveness and the one true beginning of healing. Confession is the look inward. It is a cleansing process. Just as the body heals when it detoxes, so does the bitter soul when it looks inside for what needs to be cleaned out. Forgiveness refines the look inward for truth, so we can look forward with hope. Confession is the beginning of hope because it shines the light into your internal darkness, and the darkness flees from the light, and the guilt goes with it.

Once the guilt is lifted, it will become easier to forgive others genuinely. When true forgiveness spreads through our nation, the nation will experience a wave of peace. That peace will be the sign of genuine healing. As some are healed, others will see it and want to be forgiven and healed. When the lacerations from life are mended instead of left open, righteousness and wholesomeness will be exalted over evil and debauchery. Once we let the light of truth push back the darkness, we will stop looking for political high ground to run to and begin to see the common ground we are already standing on.

Forgiveness is not only an act of obedience but is also the key to civil obedience and public order. We know what bitterness looks like, but in contrast, the picture of forgiveness is:

> The government is questioned and held accountable to the founding principles and the Constitution in real-time, not for decades or even centuries, unless it renders aid in moral, judicial, and legislative correction in the now.

> Slander, character attacks, and using someone's past against them for domination, discrediting for cancellation, gaining notoriety, or political contest are not accepted and vehemently rebuked. In place of this is the contest of ideas and visions for ways to be better.

> Foreign heads of state are respected as such, regardless of what you may think they've done wrong within their borders or between them and other countries. Making judgments based on partial truths is the same evil as presenting them.

> Posting on social media things about people, including non-edifying commentary, embarrassing or incriminating videos, pictures, and something about their past for revenge or character assassination, is considered evil and a violation of American principles. Tolerating social media slander causes the *guilty first* mentality and erodes the Sixth Amendment guarantee for us all.

> All symbols of political slant or party, hate, specific factions, subversion of the Constitution, and alienation are put away

without a government order. This means bumper stickers, yard signs, flags, etc. It also means not holding it against those who choose not to put them away.

OBEY

"Government implies the power of making laws. It is essential to the idea of a law that it be attended with a sanction; or, in other words, a penalty or punishment for disobedience. If there be no penalty annexed to disobedience, the resolutions or commands which pretend to be laws will amount to nothing more than advice or recommendation."

**—Alexander Hamilton,
The Federalist Papers, No. 15**

Obedience to the established government, with exception to immoral mandates and laws, is the essence of self-government. Republicanism is a government where leaders are *produced* and *selected* by *us* to govern. That means the people we elect are to decide on budgets, declare wars, make laws, raise and lower taxes, appoint judges and dignitaries, and maintain the common defense. The Constitution clearly outlines the organization of and selected powers and duties of government, the mechanism in which we elect leaders, and what infringements the citizens are protected from. Elected officials represent those who elect them, whether you voted for them or not. **Not only that, but obedience to the Constitution is required for survival even if the interim government doesn't; this is the rule of nations and the purpose of the First Amendment.**

The job of the citizens is to judge the government and its officials against virtue, principle, justice, and the sovereign authority of the constitution. This requires being informed and has nothing to do with opinion. It doesn't matter who you like or what you don't like about a government member, but what matters is that the laws they pass are checked against the principles and the Constitution. The following constitutional passage is an example of how the Constitution's authority and our natural form of government are disregarded:

> The United States shall guarantee to every State of this Union a Republican form of Government and shall protect them against Invasion; and on the application of the Legislature or the Executive (when the Legislature cannot be convened) against domestic Violence. *(Article IV Section 4 of The Constitution of the United States)*

If a republican form of government is constitutionally guaranteed to the states, then what are we doing defending democracy? And what is the intention of dissolving the electoral college if that is the staple of our Republican process?

The Constitution requires adherence to maintain its energy. The republic requires allegiance to retain its standing. Loyalty to the United States means putting the republic first and opinion last. To be allegiant is to put *we* before *me*. Republicanism is respect for the law, founding principles, and the Constitution. Disobedience, or allowing government disobedience, to the Constitution and our laws, especially our founding principles, are actively dismantling the country. There will always be overt and covert forces that want to dismantle a republic. Still, when patriots carry out the duty of abiding, we will be impenetrable to any foreign and domestic threat. Think regeneration, not revolution!

Rebellion disrupts the smooth flow of society, causing rogue swirls in its systems, processes, and public peace. To rebel in the little things will disrupt the big things chronically. The disorder isn't always blatant civil unrest but has many different forms, such as runaway capitalism (oligarchism), hopeless consumer debt, class warfare, perpetual armed conflict, hopeless national debt, mass reliance on subsidies, etc.

Acute lawlessness is the result of chronic godlessness and rebelliousness. The motto of the anarchists is "no god, no masters," which translates into godless lawlessness or hell on earth. Anarchism is a practice, and anarchy is a condition. Anarchy is a government without laws, where the supreme power is with each individual, who does what he wishes or has the power to do (Barton).[90] The part that says, "As each does as he wishes," should frighten anyone who would like to live in a civilized world.

Obedience is allegiance, and allegiance isn't just going with the flow, but it's enhancing the objective process and rejecting the alternate fake method of democracy. Obedience fosters respect for the laws that secure our liberty. Respect for the law is a primary civic duty and fundamental to civic peace and prosperity. In short, if you want *order*, then be *orderly*.

Duty is a responsibility, and responsibility not only comes before rights but is an immutable trade-off for rights. In other words, without the execution of duty, particularly constitutional duty, then rights, particularly constitutional rights, will cease to exist.

Unite

> "We may have all come on different ships, but we're in the same boat now."
>
> **—Martin Luther King, Jr.**[91]

The word unite is defined as "to put together to form a single unit," "to cause to adhere."[92] To be united is to be one unit or, from many, one. Unity often gets mistaken for uniform or even unionized. Uniformity is expecting everyone to be the same or have the same characteristics or viewpoints. Unionized is a collective identification for increased bargaining power against an entity or group, like the European Union, which is tied together in policy and economy, not necessarily in principle. The US is a formal union of states under one sovereign nation, which is what makes us administratively different from the EU. Unity, however, starts with seeing each other as our own. **That means one American considers the other his own regardless of their views and differences.**

Unifying as a society requires forgiveness and obedience as the norm, which is why they were put before *unite*. If the United States is to continue as a republic, then the citizenry and the government must operate in cohesion, not opposition. An informed citizenry working in close collaboration with its government is the summit of self-government.

Collusion between government and citizenry is total allegiance to the republic itself. In this setting, trust is given, as it should be, and the culture of suspicion is dissipated. The culture of collaboration and trust will thrive because the forgiveness habit insights transparency. The condition of being unified can only exist if we understand what the flag stands for. To put it bluntly, if you don't know the principles, there can be no true unity.

True unity brings proper accountability. Accountability is not only justice but also order. Truly upholding defining principles and the law of the land means not accepting deviations from the precepts and doctrines of justice. Disunity allows immorality to pervade any society and its official government, making it corrupt with a corrupt government. The pledge of allegiance says, "One nation, under God, indivisible, with liberty, and justice for all" for a reason. A nation unified in a set of moral principles and a true form of government is protected from the despair and immorality of division and partisan politics.

It is treacherous to the republic to think we must find ourselves as a nation or find new values to define us. Being united under a code of true moral virtue means that we hold ourselves accountable for upholding that code as if our survival depends on it. And as we have seen, it does depend on it.

REPEAT

> "Forgiveness is not an occasional act; it is a constant attitude."
>
> **—Martin Luther King, Jr.**[93]

The servant-leader works to develop an exceptional character, first in themselves, then in others, by intention and out of duty. The servant-leader is the lead uniter, the habitual forgiver, and honorably submissive to their government. That's why "repeat" is the last step of the "Fighting FOUR," and not "repent" or "responsibility." To repent is to *turn away from*; responsibility is the ability to respond; forgiving and obeying are the forms of repentance and responsibility that cause unity. However, for it to have any impact, it must be repeated consistently, with intentionality, and become an attitude.

When we develop an attitude of forgiveness, a spirit of moral uprightness will inevitably follow. If it is an attitude, then it will become repetitive. Consistency with the right things in our philosophy gives us a glowing character. You attract what you are, and as our character grows, it glows and draws the same out of others exposed to it. A forgiving character is an attractive character, and it is highly contagious.

As individuals, if we repeat the steps of the Fighting FOUR, our national character will begin to form into what the founders intended: a virtuous people and servant government trembling before them. As the federal character changes, the nation will be rewarded in ways we didn't know were possible. We will begin to regain control of the country, and our government will serve us instead of the oligarchs. We will see new life and life abundantly if we start now, but only if we start now.

The Call

> "We have therefore to resolve to conquer or die; Our own country's honour, all call upon us for a vigorous and manly excretion, and if we now shamefully fail, we shall become infamous to the whole world."
>
> —**George Washington** (Barton)[94]

If we don't have the attitude of intentional revival, we will give the dismantlers an inch; if you provide them with an inch, they will take a nation. This undeniable truth must be internalized, lest we become dismantlers ourselves.

The question of **Life or deathocracy** means **republicanism or democracy**. It's about keeping the form of government that was initially founded or losing the nation through the allure of *rights-based ideas* instead of *duty-first principles*.

Patriots know that allegiance means staying informed, and upholding the truth no matter how unpopular it is. They understand the concept of duty over bravado, industry over entertainment, and justice over popularity. American patriots see their country as God's mission field instead of a political battlefield and put a premium on high moral character. They see other Americans as their own and put what is best for their country before the whims and problems of foreign countries, global agendas, and their own political opinions.

There lies before us the struggle for our country, and it shall be an exertion against degeneracy, debt, debauchery, democracy, or simply *deathocracy*.

If the choice seems narrow, that's because it is.

The choice is yours, and it always was!

ENDNOTES

1   Washington, George. "Thanksgiving Proclamation (1789)." (Paragraph 1) *founders.archives.gov,* https://founders.archives.gov/documents/Washington/05-04-02-0091. Accessed 23 June 2021.

2   American Battlefield Trust. "The Battle of Monongahela." *Battlefields,* https://www.battlefields.org/learn/articles/battle-monongahela-july-9-1755. Accessed 9 June 2021.

3   Barton, David. *The Founders' Bible.* Newbury Park, CA: Shiloh Road Publishers, LLC, 2012. B1-B4.

4   Washington, George. *Farewell Address,* Govinfo.gov https://www.govinfo.gov/content/pkg/GPO-CDOC-106sdoc21/pdf/GPO-CDOC-106sdoc21.pdf. Accessed 17 June 2021.

5   Washington, George. (1783) "Sentiments on a Peace Establishment." *Press-hubs.uchicago.edu* http://press-pubs.uchicago.edu/founders/documents/a1_8_12s6.html. Accessed 10 December 2020.

6   Barton, David. (2012, 2016) *The Jefferson Lies: Exposing the Myths You've Always Believed About Thomas Jefferson.* Washington, DC: WND Books.

7   Ibid.

8   "Thomas Jefferson and the Statute for Religious Freedom." (1786), (Paragraph 3) *Virginia Museum of History and Culture,* https://www.virginiahistory.org/collections-and-resources/virginia-history-explorer/thomas-jefferson. Accessed 5 May 2020.

9   Jefferson, Thomas. "First Inaugural Address." (1801), *The Avalon Project, Yale Law School-Lillian Law Library,* https://avalon.law.yale.edu/19th_century/jefinau1.asp. Accessed 23 June 2021.

10 Jefferson, Thomas. "Second Inaugural Address." (1804), *The Avalon Project, Yale Law School-Lillian Law Library,* https://avalon.law.yale.edu/19th_century/jefinau2.asp. Accessed 23 June 2021.

11 Jefferson, Thomas. "Thomas Jefferson on Politics and Government." *Family Guardian,* https://famguardian.org/Subjects/Politics/ThomasJefferson/jeff1480.htm. Accessed 23 June 2021.

12 Jefferson, Thomas. "Thomas Jefferson to Richard Price." (1789), *Library of Congress,* loc.gov https://www.loc.gov/exhibits/jefferson/60.ht. Accessed 7 July 2021.

13 Jefferson, Thomas. "Thomas Jefferson's Top 10 Quotes on Money and Banking." *The Whitlock Co.*, whitlockco.com/thomas-jeffersons-top-10-quotes-on-money-and-banking. Accessed 23 June 2021.

14 Adams, Samuel. "John Adams > Quotes." Good Reads Inc., https://www.goodreads.com/author/quotes/1480.John_Adams. https://www.goodreads.com/author/quotes/31693.Samuel_Adams. Accessed 9 June 2021.

15 Adams, John. "John Adams > Quotes." Good Reads Inc., https://www.goodreads.com/quotes/search?utf8=%E2%9C%93&q=benjamin+rush&commit=Search. Accessed 7 July 2021.

16 Jefferson, Thomas. "Quotes on Republicanism." *AZ Quotes*, https://www.azquotes.com/quotes/topics/republicanism.html. Accessed 27 July 2021.

17 Washington, George. "Farewell Address." (Paragraph 16), *Govinfo.gov*, https://www.govinfo.gov/content/pkg/GPO-CDOC-106sdoc21/pdf/GPO-CDOC-106sdoc21.pdf. Accessed 17 June 2021.

18 Jefferson, Thomas. "Second Inaugural Address." (1804)(Paragraph 11), *The Avalon Project, Yale Law School-Lillian Law Library*, https://avalon.law.yale.edu/19th_century/jefinau2.asp. Accessed 23 June 2021.

19 Washington, George. "Farewell Address." (Paragraph 16), *Govinfo.gov*, https://www.govinfo.gov/content/pkg/GPO-CDOC-106sdoc21/pdf/GPO-CDOC-106sdoc21.pdf. Accessed 17 June 2021.

20 Washington, George. (1783) "Sentiments on a Peace Establishment." (Paragraph 10) *press-hubs.uchicago.edu*, http://press-pubs.uchicago.edu/founders/documents/a1_8_12s6.html. Accessed10 December 2020.

21 Ibid, (Paragraph 9).

22 Adams, John. "John Adams Quotes." *AZ Quotes*, https://www.azquotes.com/quote/1936. Accessed 27 July 2021.

23 Jefferson, Thomas. "Thomas Jefferson and the Statute for Religious Freedom." (1786) (1st paragraph) *Virginia Museum of History and Culture*, https://www.virginiahistory.org/collections-and-resources/virginia-history-explorer/thomas-jefferson. Accessed 5 May 2020.

24 *Definition of Freedom* [online]. Oxford University Press. 2021. Available at: https://www.lexico.com/definition/freedom. Accessed 24 June 2021.

25 Barton, David. *The Jefferson Lies: Exposing the Myths You've Always Believed About Thomas Jefferson*. Washington, DC: WND Books. 2012, 2016.

26 Barton, David. *The Founders' Bible*. Newbury Park, CA: Shiloh Road Publishers, LLC, 2012. 82-84.

27 Barton, David. *The Jefferson Lies: Exposing the Myths You've Always Believed About Thomas Jefferson*. Washington, DC: WND Books. 2012, 2016.

28 O'Connell, Robert L. *Fierce Patriot: The Tangled Lives of William Tecumseh Sherman*, New York: Random House. 2012.

29 Ibid.

30 Ibid.

31 "Civil War Casualties." *American Battlefield Trust,* battlefields.org,https://www.battlefields.org/learn/articles/civil-war-casualties. Accessed 24 June 2021.

32 Faust, Drew Gilpin. *This Republic of Suffering: Death and the American Civil War.* New York: Alfred A. Knopf; Toronto, Canada: Random House of Canada Limited. 2008.

33 O'Connell, Robert L. *Fierce Patriot: The Tangled Lives of William Tecumseh Sherman*, New York: Random House. 2012.

34 *Definition of Despotism* [online]. Oxford University Press. 2021. Available at: https://www.lexico.com/en/definition/despotism. Accessed 1 July 2021.

35 *Definition of Opinion* [online]. Oxford University Press. 2021. Available at: https://www.lexico.com/en/definition/opinion. Accessed 1 July 2021.

36 Adams, Samuel. "Samuel Adams > Quotes." *Good Reads Inc.,* https://www.goodreads.com/author/quotes/31693.Samuel_Adams. Accessed 9 June 2021

37 Jefferson, Thomas. "Second Inaugural Address." (1804), (Paragraph 11) *The Avalon Project, Yale Law School- Lillian Law Library.*

38 Ibid, (paragraph 16).

39 [KFCrazy]. (2010, October 12), "The Patriot" go to war debate [Video file]. Retrieved from https://youtu.be/EGgaXXBkE8A. (1:02-1:10).

40 Jefferson, Thomas. (1787), "Extract from Thomas Jefferson to William Stephens Smith." *Jefferson Quotes and Family Letters*, Thomas Jefferson Foundation, Th. Jefferson Monticello, http://tjrs.monticello.org/letter/100. Accessed 1 January 2021.

41 Plato. 380 BC, Translated by Benjamin Jowett *The Republic*, New York, NY: Open Road Integrated Media, Inc. 2014.

42 Washington, George. "Farewell Address." (Paragraph 33) *Govinfo.gov* https://www.govinfo.gov/content/pkg/GPO-CDOC-106sdoc21/pdf/GPO-CDOC-106sdoc21.pdf. Accessed 17 June 2021.

43 Ibid, (Paragraph 33).

44 Jefferson, Thomas. "Second Inaugural Address." (Paragraph 4) *The Avalon Project, Yale Law School-Lillian Law Library,* https://avalon.law.yale.edu/19th_century/jefinau2.asp. Accessed 23 June 2021. 1804.

45 Madison, James. "James Madison > Quotes." *Good Reads Inc.,* https://www.goodreads.com/quotes/search?commit=Search&page=2&q=James+Madison+&utf8=%E2%9C%93. Accessed 23 June 2021. 1795.

46 [National Archives]. (2011, January 19), *Eisenhower's 'Military-Industrial Complex' Speech Origins and Significance,* [Video file]. Retrieved from https://youtu.be/Gg-jvHynP9Y.

47 Adams, John. "John Adams > Quotes." *AZ Quotes*, https://www.azquotes.com/quote/1311372. Accessed 7 July 2021.

48 Adams, Samuel. "Samuel Adams > Quote." *Good Reads Inc.*, https://www.goodreads.com/author/quotes/31693.Samuel_Adams. Accessed 9 June 2021)

49 "2019 National Veteran Suicide Prevention Report Office of Mental Health and Suicide Prevention USDVA." *mentalhealth.va.gov*, https://www.mentalhealth.va.gov/docs/data-sheets/2019/2019_National_Veteran_Suicide_Prevention_Annual_Report_508.pdf.

50 "Suicide Statistics." *American Foundation for Suicide Prevention* (AFSP.ORG) https://afsp.org/suicide-statistics. Accessed 11 July 2021.

51 Rickards, James. *Currency Wars: The Making of the Next Global Crisis*, New York, NY: Penguin. 2011.

52 Ibid.

53 "Be Informed: National Debt." *Just Facts*, https://www.justfacts.com/nationaldebt.asp. Accessed 9 July 2021.

54 "U.S Defense Spending Compared To Other Nations." *Peter G. Peterson Foundation*, pgpf.org, https://www.pgpf.org/chart-archive/0053_defense-comparison. Accessed 12 July 2021.

55 "Foreign Aid By Country: Who Is Getting The Most—And How Much?" *Concern Worldwide USA, Inc.*, concernusa.org https://www.concernusa.org/story/foreign-aid-by-country/?utm_source=grgs&utm_medium=cpc&utm_campaign=bsd-gsgr-awar-infocontent&utm_content=v3&utm_term=foreign-aid&c_src=grgs-cpc&c_src2=bsd-gsgr-awar-infocontent-foreign-aid-v3&gclid=CjwKCAjwjJmIBhA4EiwAQdCbxhCET21_WamOWE2ezme LUDBbTHQyiWnMOyIJQJvSMG0hV5RGuwM8rRoC3CoQAvD_BwE.

56 "Drug Overdose Death Statistics." *National Center for Drug Abuse Statistics*, drugabusstatistics .org https://drugabusestatistics.org/drug-overdose-deaths. Accessed 12 July 2021.

57 "National Health Care Expenditure Data." *NHE Fact Sheet*, cms.gov, https://www.cms.gov/Research-Statistics-Data-and-Systems/Statistics-Trends-and-Reports/NationalHealthExpendData/NHE-Fact-Sheet. Accessed July 2021.

58 Tikkanen, Roosa and Melinda K. Abrams. (January 2020), "U.S. Health Care From a Global Perspective; Higher Spending, Worse Outcomes?" *The Commonwealth Fund*, comonwealthfund.org, https://www.commonwealthfund.org/publications/issue-briefs/2020/jan/us-health-care-global-perspective-2019?gclid=Cj0KCQjw0K-HBhDDARIsAFJ6UGg5B0rq6OuZGcEC_vU1lNB_XTWBNsfFqNcuwneGyPNpQ8cMqXhXJlAaAoV5EALw_wcB. Accessed 19 July 2021.

59 "National Health Care Expenditure Data." *NHE Fact Sheet*, https://www.cms. gov/Research-Statistics-Data-and-Systems/Statistics-Trends-and-Reports/ NationalHealthExpendData/NHE-Fact-Sheet. Accessed 12 July 2021.

60 Brenan, Megan. "Support for Legal Marijuana Inches Up to 68%." *Gallup, Inc.,* https://news.gallup.com/poll/323582/support-legal-marijuana-inches-new-high.aspx. Accessed 21 July 2021. 9 November 2020.

61 DISA Global Solutions. "Wondering what the law is in your state." *disa.com*, https://disa.com/map-of-marijuana-legality-by-state. Accessed 21 July 2021. 2021.

62 National Center for Drug Abuse Statistics. (NCDAS), "Marijuana." *drugabusestatistics.org*, https://drugabusestatistics.org/. Accessed 21 July 2021.

63 National Center for Drug Abuse Statistics. (NCDAS), "Marijuana use among youth." *drugabusestatistics.org*, https://drugabusestatistics.org/marijuana-addiction/. Accessed 21 July 2021.

64 IBID

65 Yakowicz, Will. "U.S. Cannabis Sales Hit Record $17.5 Billion As Americans Consume More Marijuana Than Ever Before." *Forbes*, https://www.forbes. com/sites/willyakowicz/2021/03/03/us-cannabis-sales-hit-record-175-billion-as-americans-consume-more-marijuana-than-ever-before/?sh=1400f6162bcf. Accessed 21 July 2021. 3 March 2021.

66 National Center for Drug Abuse Statistics. (NCDAS), "Drug Use Among Youth: Facts & Statistics/Marijuana Abuse." *drugabusestatistics.org*, https:// drugabusestatistics.org/teen-drug-use/. Accessed 21 July 2021.

67 National Center for Drug Abuse Statistics. (NCDAS), "Drug Use Among Youth: Facts & Statistics/Drug Abuse Among Youth." *drugabusestatistics.org*, https://drugabusestatistics.org/teen-drug-use/. Accessed 21 July 2021.

68 National Center for Drug Abuse Statistics. (NCDAS), "Marijuana Addiction: Rates & Usage Statistics, Legalization of Marijuana." *drugabusestatistics.org*, https://drugabusestatistics.org/marijuana-addiction/. Accessed 21 July 2021.

69 Yakowicz, Will. "U.S. Cannabis Sales Hit Record $17.5 Billion As Americans Consume More Marijuana Than Ever Before." *Forbes*, https://www.forbes. com/sites/willyakowicz/2021/03/03/us-cannabis-sales-hit-record-175-billion-as-americans-consume-more-marijuana-than-ever-before/?sh=1400f6162bcf. Accessed 21 July 2021. 3 March 2021.

70 National Center for Drug Abuse Statistics. (NCDAS), "Marijuana Addiction: Rates & Usage Statistics, Highlights." *drugabusestatistics.com*, https:// drugabusestatistics.org/marijuana-addiction/,marijuana. Accessed 21 July 2021.

71 National Center for Drug Abuse Statistics. (NCDAS), "Use Among Youth: Facts and Statistics, Report Highlights." *drugabusestatistics.com,* https://drugabusestatistics.org/teen-drug-use/,drug.

72 Covenant Eyes. "PornStats: 250+ Facts, Quotes, and Statistics about Pornography Use." *Covenant Eyes, Inc.,* available @ https://www.covenanteyes.com/e-books/. 6. 2018.

73 Ibid, 28.

74 Dugan, Andrew. "More Americans Say Pornography Is Morally Acceptable." *Gallup, Inc.,* https://news.gallup.com/poll/235280/americans-say-pornography-morally-acceptable.aspx. Accessed 21 July 2021. 5 June 2018.

75 Foubert, John. "How Much do Pornographers Make?" *JohnFoubert.com,* https://www.johnfoubert.com/how-much-do-pornographers-make.

76 Benes, Ross. "Porn could have a bigger economic influence on the U.S. than Netflix, Yahoo! Finance." *finance.yahoo.com,* https://finance.yahoo.com/news/porn-could-bigger-economic-influence-121524565.html. Accessed 21 July 2021. 20 June 2018.

77 Froubert, John D. "How Many people use pornography." *johnfroubert.com,* https://www.johnfoubert.com/how-many-people-use-porn. Accessed 21 July 2021. 2021.

78 Brinlee, Morgan. "13 Sex Trafficking Statistics That Put The Worldwide Problem into Perspective." *bustle.com,* Bustle (magazine) https://www.bustle.com/p/13-sex-trafficking-statistics-that-put-the-worldwide-problem-into-perspective-9930150. 30 July 2018.

79 Plato. 380 BC, Translated by Benjamin Jowett *The Republic,* New York, NY: Open Road Integrated Media, Inc. 2014.

80 Barton, David. *The Founders' Bible.* Newbury Park, CA: Shiloh Road Publishers, LLC, 147. 2012.

81 Jefferson, Thomas. "Thomas Jefferson Quotes." *Brainy Quote,* https://www.brainyquote.com/authors/thomas-jefferson-quotes.

82 *Definition of Principle* [online]. Oxford University Press. Available at: https://www.lexico.com/definition/freedom. Accessed 21 July 2021. 2021.

83 *Definition of Truth* [online]. Merriam-Webster. Available at: https://www.merriam-webster.com/dictionary/truth. Accessed 21 July 2021. 2021.

84 Barton, David. *The Founders' Bible.* Newbury Park, CA: Shiloh Road Publishers, LLC, 2012. 1877.

85 Washington, George. "Farewell Address." 27, *Govinfo.gov,* https://www.govinfo.gov/content/pkg/GPO-CDOC-106sdoc21/pdf/GPO-CDOC-106sdoc21.pdf. Accessed 17 June 2021.

86 Barton, David. *The Founders' Bible.* Newbury Park, CA: Shiloh Road Publishers, LLC, 2012. 1877.

87   Barton, David. *The Founders' Bible*. Newbury Park, CA: Shiloh Road Publishers, LLC, 2012. 187.

88   Washington, George. "Farewell Address." 27, *Govinfo.gov,* https://www. govinfo.gov/content/pkg/GPO-CDOC-106sdoc21/pdf/GPO-CDOC-106sdoc21.pdf. Accessed 17 June 2021.

89   King, Jr., Martin Luther. "Martin Luther King, Jr Quotes About Forgiveness." *azquotes.com,*   https://www.azquotes.com/author/8044-Martin_Luther_ King_Jr/tag/forgiveness. Accessed 26 July 2021.

90   Barton, David. *The Founders' Bible*. Newbury Park, CA: Shiloh Road Publishers, LLC, 2012. 147.

91   King, Jr., Martin Luther. "Martin Luther King, Jr Quotes." *brainy quote. com,* https://www.brainyquote.com/quotes/martin_luther_king_jr_132359. Accessed 26 July 2021.

92   Definition of Unite [online]. Merriam-Webster. 2020.Available at: https:// www.merriam-webster.com/dictionary/unite Accessed 2 November 2020.

93   Barton, David. *The Founders' Bible*. Newbury Park, CA: Shiloh Road Publishers, LLC, 2012. 431.